I0801484

# COMMENTARY ON SINGAPORE

## ❷ Economy, Environment and Population

# COMMENTARY ON SINGAPORE

## ❷ Economy, Environment and Population

Edited by

**Gillian Koh**

National University of Singapore Society, Singapore

NUSS
The Graduate Club

World Scientific

*Published by*

World Scientific Publishing Co. Pte. Ltd.
5 Toh Tuck Link, Singapore 596224
*USA office:* 27 Warren Street, Suite 401-402, Hackensack, NJ 07601
*UK office:* 57 Shelton Street, Covent Garden, London WC2H 9HE

**National Library Board, Singapore Cataloguing in Publication Data**
Name(s): Koh, Gillian, editor.
Title: Commentary on Singapore / edited by Gillian Koh.
Description: Singapore : World Scientific Publishing Co. Pte. Ltd., [2024]
Identifier(s): ISBN 978-981-12-6454-2 (hardcover ; volume 1) |
ISBN 978-981-12-6559-4 (paperback ; volume 1) |
ISBN 978-981-12-6455-9 (ebook for institutions ; volume 1) |
ISBN 978-981-12-6456-6 (ebook for individuals ; volume 1) |
ISBN 978-981-12-8106-8 (hardcover ; volume 2) |
ISBN 978-981-12-8139-6 (paperback ; volume 2) |
ISBN 978-981-12-8107-5 (ebook for institutions ; volume 2) |
ISBN 978-981-12-8108-2 (ebook for individuals ; volume 2) |
ISBN 978-981-12-8703-9 (hardcover ; volume 3) |
ISBN 978-981-12-8732-9 (paperback ; volume 3) |
ISBN 978-981-12-8704-6 (ebook for institutions ; volume 3) |
ISBN 978-981-12-8705-3 (ebook for individuals ; volume 3)
Subject(s): LCSH: Singapore--History. | Singapore--Politics and government. |
Singapore--Foreign relations. | Singapore--Economic policy. | Environmental policy--Singapore. |
Singapore--Population. | Singapore--Social policy.
Classification: DDC 959.57--dc23

**British Library Cataloguing-in-Publication Data**
A catalogue record for this book is available from the British Library.

Copyright © 2024 by NUSS

*All rights reserved.*

For any available supplementary material, please visit
https://www.worldscientific.com/worldscibooks/10.1142/13535#t=suppl

Desk Editor: Jiang Yulin

Typeset by Stallion Press
Email: enquiries@stallionpress.com

Printed in Singapore

# Mission Statement

*"To foster a lifelong relationship with NUS and the wider graduate community."*

At NUSS, a lifelong relationship with NUS and the wider graduate community is achieved through two mutually reinforcing thrusts:

- Promoting the interests of its members and NUS; and
- Contributing positively to Singapore's political and intellectual development and helping to cultivate a more gracious social and cultural environment.

As the foremost graduate society, NUSS strives to promote the interests of its stakeholders by providing appropriate platforms for all to socialise, build networks, improve connectivity and exchange ideas through a multitude of recreational, academic, political, social and cultural activities.

# Contents

# Introduction

What you have in your hand is the second of a three-volume set of essays we hope will inform thought and debate on Singapore's future.

The essays were first published in the National University of Singapore Society's (NUSS) journal called *Commentary* which has drawn on thought-leadership across Singapore over several years on topics of Singapore's political, economic, social and cultural development as well as foreign relations.

The journal has several objectives that are an extension of those of NUSS itself — to promote the continued intellectual development of its membership as well as to enable the membership to foster a gracious social and cultural environment.

NUSS and the *Commentary* team felt that in this age of rapid change not only in Singapore but the world, there were many essays in past editions of the journal that can continue to provide intellectual ballast as well as provocation for fresh thinking on governance and public policy to the broader Singaporean public as they have done for its membership.

This volume has been curated to focus on the areas of economic policy, the environment and demography. These seem like disparate topics at first glance. But publishing this in 2024 with what is now a widespread and even acute consciousness around the concept of sustainability, we hope readers find that this combination makes eminent sense.

For an explicit statement of how this is so, start at the end of this book with Chapter 13 by young social entrepreneur Veerappan Swaminathan. He introduces the "Three Pillars Model of Sustainability" that sets out how the economy, the environment and society are interconnected. We are reminded that the environment is the finite boundary within which society and the economy exist. The economy is a subset of, or exists within society as it is created by people for the exchange of labour, value, products and services. It is important to emphasise that society is much larger than the economy as many people are not part of the latter — think of the unpaid caregivers and stay-at-home mums, Veerappan says.

He makes the sharp point about life in Singapore today — "we tend to give outsized attention and dedicate immense resources to the economy, with society being deemed as being of secondary importance, and the environment often relegated to an occasional concern." Instead, he argues, each is interrelated, with the health of one pillar or sphere, affecting the other pillars.

As an island-state, we are conscious of two things: First, that we have to take the best care we can of our own bio- or ecological sphere. Second, that we do borrow, buy, or depend on the bio- or ecological sphere of so many other countries. Everything we live on is imported and a third of our economy is driven by foreign labour too. This often results in us believing that we have the license to take advantage of these resources from bio- or ecological sphere of others — we have no choice, we tell ourselves. However, it is safe to say that we have been conscious of the need to do the first and performed it as best we can. If that is the case, we can also well afford to and know how to do our part as global citizens to take care of the world around us as we are dependent on the well-being of the countries around us too.

The people question has also been front and centre of the economic and environmental question. As a country that came into being unexpectedly, it lost its hinterland and had just two key assets to count on — its people and its geographical location. With a new nation that existed for a culturally diverse population as its only *raison d'être*, Singapore had to provide a sustainable livelihood for 1.887 million people at the time of Independence.

This takes us straight to the first chapter by Tan Khee Giap, Evan Tan and Vincent Kwan which provides a comprehensive review of the history of economic development in independent Singapore with a useful comparative analysis of Malaysia and Hong Kong. More specifically, they do that by setting potential growth against actualised performance of these economies to set up a discussion about the factors behind the different development experiences across them. Put simply, pragmatic policy — efficiently and honestly implemented — has helped Singapore do better than the relatively well-resourced Malaysia. Over the past five decades, a more market-attuned and leaner, ironically, less-welfarist government has allowed Singapore to perform better than "laissez-faire Hong Kong" also even with its large Chinese hinterland. The data and statistical analyses of the three economies, even through the boom and busts of regional and global crises, provide useful reference points in this opening chapter of the volume.

The other enduring value of the essay lies in the questions the authors articulate about Singapore's growth potential, and these continue to be relevant in 2024 and many more years to come. These questions amply demonstrate an appreciation of the interaction of the economy with environment and society but also an acute sense of public sentiment that prevails in relation to these: The first question is whether Singapore's economy has grown "too fast", beyond its natural and social limits that will compromise the liveability of the city and the meaningful inclusion of Singaporeans in it. This issue of whether driving high-octane growth rates on the back of rapid structural transformation and massive intake of foreign labour, the resulting congestion, and rising income disparity truly translate into long-term and deep benefit to Singaporeans has been raised. This lay at the heart of a highly-contested general election in 2011 when the political opposition wrested a high watermark of six seats in Parliament as Singaporeans expressed their ambivalence about the implications of such strategies on that broader notion of "sustainability".

Tan et al. argue that being an open economy, Singapore is highly vulnerable to the vagaries of the global economy and therefore has little choice but to ride favourable waves of development when possible. This is to shore up its resources that will help it ride out the storm when it occurs. They also recognise that more discussion will be needed around not just the reskilling of labour but providing broader social support to mitigate income divides or dislocation of labour. As such, the second question they raise is whether the political system is capable of providing a workable public consensus on these issues of immigration, social support, and the most effective and sustainable growth strategies for the particular case of our small open economy. While a fresh "social contract" will be needed, their plea is that Singaporeans will not be "inward-looking" but take the global perspective into consideration. They hope that citizen participation in this process will not lead to conflict, government gridlock, or a bloated government.

David Skilling's essay in Chapter 2 reinforces the notion that small states like Singapore face particular constraints in delivering long-term growth and development for their people. Recognising that Singapore very effectively took advantage of two factors — the global multilateral order and the demographic dividend of the large number of youthful citizens entering into the workforce in the past five decades, he brings more specific strategies to the discussion.

With the weakening of the rules-based multilateral order and rising trade tensions between the United States and China, the global context has changed. In 2024, most accept that these are now full-blown geopolitical and economic disruptions. Yet, the opportunities for moving to a new technological frontier of industrial and business development that is web-based and artificial intelligence-driven are also tremendous. These present special opportunities — the digital economy can get around some of the constraints Singapore has faced. While advanced economies should expect a more mature rate of 2 to 3 percent growth in gross domestic product (GDP) per annum, he suggests three thrusts Singapore can adopt, building on the "hub of hubs" strategy that the Government has successfully pursued in the now dimming age of globalisation.

The first is to create critical mass and deep, dense, reinforcing economic activities around just a selected number of new industries to reduce the exposure to footloose capital. These activities must sink big roots to become critical nodes to the global value chain.

Second, Singapore firms should take the same approach to linking up with the region. At the time of writing, Skilling noted that Singapore's export share to ASEAN was merely 20 percent which suggests a lot more headroom to tie itself into its immediate region through trade and investment.

Third, and considering the higher level of volatility that small states are subject to, as noted by Tan et al. earlier, Skilling makes the point that a higher level of "social insurance" will be needed for Singaporeans. Certainly no one would argue against ensuring that the fruits of economic development are better distributed across society, but the new point here is that this must also help to allocate risk more efficiently across the economy. An economy driven by the latest in technology, that rewards innovation and creativity, will also mean that there will be new sets of losers — those who take the wrong bets or where the ideas just do not work. Social insurance provides the safety net that allows entrepreneurs and workers to move into emerging areas of activity with the knowledge that such risks are managed or mitigated. It allows the broader public to support economic transformation as the pain of disruption is mitigated.

Again, if the economy exists for the people and not the other way around, if it is designed to allow for the flourishing of human potential, then this is meaningful. But it is a point of difference between Skilling and Tan et. al. This argument provides context for the policy reforms that are on-going under the fourth generation of government leaders' Forward Singapore exercise of 2022–2023 to look at the evolution of the social compact between state and citizens, and among citizens with each other. More social risk-pooling frameworks are in place through the upgraded Central Provident Fund system, greater provision has been made for paid training and work placement schemes by the Government, and more substantial transfer payments through income support for low-wage workers through the Workfare Scheme are now available. There are signals that more policy changes are in the offing.

This is the right juncture at which to introduce Chapter 11 by Paul Cheung on Demography. He records the sentiment, rife at the point of writing, that citizens felt they lacked "home-court advantage"; that "they are disadvantaged and discriminated against in their home country". This perception, he explains, arose because of long-term and increasingly aggressive moves to introduce foreigners to augment Singapore's population and workforce which had suffered from an all-too-effective anti-natalist policy Cheung himself was tasked to reverse in 1987 as Director of the government's Population Planning Unit. Singaporeans' perception, he argues, was that they were being squeezed down in their wages by the large number of foreigners in the workplace and squeezed out in their bid for housing, access to public services, and the daily necessities of life.

On the other hand, the recommendations of Skilling, Cheung and even Susana Harding in Chapter 12 on greater social support for the bourgeoning population of seniors in particular, shore up that sense of a shared future, stakeholdership, and solidarity that seems to be lacking according to Cheung.

The transition to new economic activity and business models, the required talent, skills, and labour profile means that the dislocation of workers is inevitable. The government, a reflection of popular will, must provide the necessary support. How quickly can these transitions happen? If the ramifications for "society" and "environment" are important, what support is needed to ensure that the upside of these policies outweighs the downside, and how long an effort will be needed to arrive at a new equilibrium? Will the rewards be great enough to afford the necessary expansion of social support? In the final reckoning, will this be fiscally sustainable and reinforce the strength of society and its people, or erode it?

The fine balance across the three pillars of sustainability are well-captured too in Chapter 3 by Piyush Gupta in the case study of the development of Singapore as a financial hub and its useful discussion of how talent and manpower policies moved in tandem with the impetus for Singapore to capitalise on a "time-zone advantage" to achieve that status of being a global hub. This would provide critical auxiliary support services to its trading activities. In the latter years, the market chose Singapore as trusted host to a range of wealth management players that serve the emerging Southeast Asian region. Gupta argues for the need to build up a strong core of Singaporean specialists and leaders of influence in these fields to permanently anchor itself within these highly profitable value chains of financial activity; that active policy is needed to ensure that Singapore and Singaporeans benefit from these developments.

Yet again, Chapter 4 by Laurence Liew reinforces the point about social sustainability and resilience even in the midst of economic transformation as he provides this volume with insights into the first of the three newer or unfolding areas of technological and economic development — Industrial Revolution 4.0. In this new world of pervasive digitalisation and artificial intelligence (AI), Liew explains how the compact between government and its people and between industries and its workers will also be revolutionised.

While these trends will allow workers to focus on higher-order, higher value-added work that only humans can perform, the process of learning to leverage the technology will take time. He notes that Singapore must do two things to ensure that people are served by the economy and not the other way around. One, is what was already being introduced with the first wave of the transition: generous schemes are offered, like income, to those who are training and apply those skills at AI Singapore which Liew leads. These can be "universalised" to all workers as these technologies are propagated across sectors. This would be superior to the idea of providing citizens with a "universal basic income" that seeks to provide merely subsistence income to a population as the alternative. Support comes with the upskilling process, which, it is assumed will lead people to better jobs.

The second thing is the imperative of designing new applications or uses of the technology around open-source code. This is to ensure that technopreneurship — the prospect of developing new innovations, and with that new wealth creation, diffuse as far and wide as possible. The spectre of robots taking over the world and humans subsisting on basic income with not much else to do, as portrayed in the 2018 film, Ready Player One, is certainly far from Liew's vision of a Singapore that rides on the wave of IR 4.0.

After ChatGPT was launched in 2022, more thoughtful individuals and certainly those operating in the world of AI have been thinking through the economic, ethical and regulatory implications of these developments. It is good to know that Singapore launched A.I.Verify which is Governance Testing and Framework Toolkit in 2022 to enable developers to self-test as well as allow others to validate with transparency, an AI system's claims about its approach, use and outcomes — its trustworthiness to consumers and its impact on society.

The second emerging trend is tackled by Dr Sanchita Basu Das in Chapter 5. She touches on the diffusion of digitalisation, this time, across Southeast Asia. There are vast growth opportunities in helping this region of emerging markets adopt this technology in the areas of transportation, the environment, health, and more. The introduction of web-enabled commerce in the private sector but also digitally-enabled trade facilitation, logistical services, and customs facilitation can allow several countries to leap-frog into the future. This is as long as there is an effort to build up the digital capabilities of our neighbours. With the propagation of digital economy agreements (DEAs), that adoption, collaboration and innovation from cities to farms, are made possible between Singapore and its neighbours. It is in fact, the only way to achieve the network benefits of the digital economy. The returns accrue only when adoption happens at scale. Today, Singapore has bilateral DEAs with four countries. The country also continues to support the completion of a study on an ASEAN Digital Economy Framework Agreement that should have been completed in 2023 to guide negotiation for the agreement so that it can be concluded in 2025.

The third trend and perhaps the most critical of them is in the realm of energy and its direct impact on sustainability and climate change. Here, Lee Tzu Yang who was the former chairman of Shell Companies in Singapore describes the transition that Singapore has been making towards the use of liquified national gas (LNG), perhaps the least pollutive of fossil fuels in terms of carbon emissions per unit of electricity. He also describes how Singapore has been gunning to be Southeast Asia's hub for gas. He notes that Singapore took the initiative in 2006 to build a world-class regasification terminal which was completed in 2013. The second move was to set up a robust set of regulations, pricing frameworks, financial infrastructure, and relevant specialist talent to create this new industry. This was viewed as being the next best thing to stepping away from more polluting forms of energy generation, given that Singapore is "renewables-deficient".

In 2023, 95 percent of Singapore's electricity was indeed generated from piped natural gas (PNG) and LNG when it was merely 19 percent in 2000. When the demand for energy rose as major economies emerged from the COVID-19 pandemic and supplies were disrupted with production problems in PNG in West Natuna and South Sumatra, and the start of the Russia–Ukraine War in February 2022, prices have risen drastically. However, in October 2021, the Government was able to establish a "Standby LNG Facility" or a ready supply of LNG, which electricity generation companies (gencos) can draw on. It also modified market rules to allow the Energy Market Authority to direct these gencos to draw on this LNG if their supplies of natural gas are disrupted, to provide price stability to their consumers. This has helped stave off precipitous rise in energy prices and cost of living in Singapore.

In April 2022, Second Minister for Trade and Industry, Dr Tan See Leng stated that the decision to build an LNG terminal had allowed Singapore to tap gas sources further afield and provide sufficient capacity to meet all of Singapore's natural gas needs should PNG be unavailable. This facility has made for a greater measure of energy resilience generally. Looking to the future however, the Government has stated that natural gas is but one of four sources of energy that also take into consideration the imperative of minimising the country's carbon footprint. The other three are solar power; low carbon alternatives like green hydrogen; and the development and tapping of regional renewable energy grids. This chapter by Lee was written at an "historic, inflexion point" in the energy story for both Singapore and Southeast Asia — in 2014 and how right he was as the issues raised continue to play out now and even more so with the disruption to energy supplies with current Russia–Ukraine War. The author has chosen to add a short epilogue to the essay.

This challenge of acting to support climate sustainability is acutely felt as this volume is being compiled. The United Nations (UN) Intergovernmental Panel on Climate Change issued its sixth and final comprehensive, scientific assessment in March 2023. It states that human activities, principally through the emissions of greenhouse gases, have "unequivocally caused global warming", where the average surface temperature of the planet has risen 1.1 degrees Celsius above that of the pre-Industrial period, 1850–1900, in the years between 2011 and 2020.

This has resulted in weather and climate extremes witnessed across the globe. It also takes our habitat close to the 1.5-degree Celsius threshold beyond which scientists have warned would result in severely discontinuous, devastating self-reinforcing climate change loops like the complete and irreversible melting of the ice-caps, the rising of sea-levels, changes in the salinity levels of the oceans and as a result, shifts in mega-tidal currents and wind patterns. Liveability, food production, and broader human security could be in peril.

Singapore has grasped the magnitude of the problem even if, using UN's measures, it contributes only 0.11 percent to carbon emissions globally. It is an outsized effect for a small city-state that is a result of its bunkering activities where the final consumers are elsewhere. In February 2021, the Government introduced a multi-ministry Singapore Green Plan 2030 that seeks to galvanise all the stakeholders in the country — government, business, people — around the ambition of bringing the country's carbon emissions to a peak in 2030 and halving them by 2050. In October 2022, the Government committed Singapore to a more ambitious target of achieving net zero carbon emissions by 2050, ahead of the UN COP27 Climate Change Conference in Egypt.

Within this context, this volume re-publishes four important essays from past editions of *Commentary* on the Environment. Chapter 7 by Kenneth Er and Leong Chee Chiew is the twin to Chapter 1 with its review of the five-decade national strategy to achieve an important balance between environmental sustainability with economic development. It provides a record of the intentional strategy of mitigating pollution but also of developing nature as a partner in the drive towards industralisation. As Dr Geh Min puts it in Chapter 8, it is remarkable and visionary that the Government, and in particular, the founding PM, Lee Kuan Yew, saw the cleaning and greening of the country as a necessary component to its economic strategy.

Er and Leong explain how the greening movement was launched in 1963 as an economic and social imperative — to differentiate Singapore from other developing countries so that it would not suffer from wanton pollution by industry, but also provide a statement of the country's national brand in how it could discipline the development of the city and economy to considerations of ecology and urban planning.

This sense of "environmental possibilism" and successful implementation of the vision of making Singapore a "Garden City", to being a "City in a Garden" and now, a "City in Nature", lies in first, the active and even personal attention that has been given to the strategy by the political leader. Second, the institutional arrangement of having the ministry responsible of national infrastructural development and not the environment lead the charge framed the national strategy correctly. Third, resources were put into developing the professional capabilities of talent and manpower to sustain the growth and maintenance of this Garden City. This provided the impetus to experiment and innovate around the landscaping and environmental sustainability industries. Fourth, it has been important to recognise that the community plays an integral role in all these plans. This, especially as the visions of being a City in a Garden or City in Nature necessarily mean that the people have a sense of ownership and direct connection with nature. Er and Leong cite many initiatives to foster this. From inculcating the gardening culture even in public housing estates through the promotion of community gardens to activating "citizen scientists" to record and promote nature conservation, these cultivate the idea that every action can uphold or undermine our ecological health. These, hopefully, will help to re-orientate stakeholders away from just the utilitarian and pragmatic view of nature to an appreciation of it for its own sake; it should tip the balance between consumerism and conservation as the other authors in this section note is central to the drive towards sustainability.

This difference in approach, or environmental identity, is what Leong Ching explains in Chapter 10. She notes that Singaporeans are more anthropocentric as they adopt an instrumentalist approach to nature than ecocentric where people find inherent value in nature and feel it is worth preserving for its own sake. The problem of food wastage in Singapore reflects this anthropocentric nature. It is also why recycling rates are not where they ought to be. It is also why water conservation has generally required the use of the pricing mechanism before more optimal levels of use can be achieved.

The authors in the section highlight the challenges that Singapore will have to face — some are long-standing ones and others are emerging. The key points to note from Dr Geh's chapter are, first that Singapore needs to improve on its capacity to collect, analyse, interpret and apply objective appraisals of its environmental record. It should do this as well as it does with economic performance, she argues. This is necessary for future planning of urban and infrastructural redevelopment. At the time of writing, she also decried the lack of regulatory provision that environmental impact assessments are needed for such work. Even the 2013 plans for land use and population growth of the Government lacked such rigour, as is also the case with specific projects including those related to flood control and climate change adaptation, she argues. Regional and international disputes will require this capacity for us to represent and defend our rights, she adds.

In citing the regional "haze" problem that stems from the slash and burn practices of clearing forests as well as the sheer effect of drier climate primarily in Indonesia, green accounting should facilitate a more accurate assessment of the ecological impact if not also the social impact of business practices.

In addition, Dr Geh highlights how important industrial and human security infrastructure — think of our financial centre, airport and the petrochemical hub on Jurong Island — are built on low-lying reclaimed land and could be compromised in a era of climate change. This is the case with many urban centres in Southeast Asia too. If all these are distressed, we can envisage a scenario of mass migration in the region. Just as the economic and energy stories are tied to the region, so is the ecological one.

More critically, Dr Geh warns that Singapore must act on these scenarios. Otherwise, the Singapore brand would change from that of an economic high-flyer to an "environmental freeloader" — an epitaph that the successful execution of the Green Plan should help the country avoid.

In that regard, economist Euston Quah's essay with Christabelle Soh in Chapter 9, is useful. While it sets out what seems to be trade-offs — it has always seemed like being economically competitive meant that environmental sustainability had to be compromised, they remind us that the longer-term costs for neglecting the environment are high as these undermine competitiveness. Perhaps the truly cheapest and easiest way ahead would be to rely on renewable energy by developing the regional power grid aggressively. But the trade-off of Singapore being dependent on that, they argue, is security.

Therefore, Quah and Soh speak of the need to decouple growth from energy which is where productivity and certainly green technologies fit in. They also speak of the need to decouple growth from waste which is where the 3Rs of reduce, reuse, recycle fit in. Finally, over the long term, concerns about growth inevitably lead to debates about manpower and the population policy that have the knock-on effects on liveability too.

Their plea is to re-estimate what is the optimal balance of population size, energy demand, the fuel mix, waste, with the objective that is not the pursuit of economic growth that should define these efforts of development but the higher order notion of achieving "quality of life". The end goal of the country should be to attain that and not merely levels of GDP.

From that perspective, the dilemmas about demography and the appropriate population size for city-state Singapore can be more clearly appreciated and even, resolved. In Chapter 11 on Singapore's demographic future, Cheung provides the projections of population decline depending on the size at which immigration is permitted or relied on. If not for these strategies to augment the younger, working age segments of the population, economic performance would wane, Cheung argues. Immigration to keep the proportion of working-age people constant would require more effort in the promotion of family formation and far greater acceptance for a foreign population in the country. If the strategy is to achieve "quality growth" rather than "to grow at all cost" to facilitate human development, environmental sustainability and social inclusion, those dilemmas about population augmentation, the choice of industry, and ultimately, the right rate of economic growth do need to be revisited.

Chapter 12 by Susana Harding provides another facet to the national development strategy — how well can we age as individuals and citizens in Singapore, and how well can we really live? Can people age-in-place and not feel that they must dislodge themselves from the homes of their youth; to downsize and lose their community. Surely, to live well is to be able to age well. When it comes down to it, true "sustainability" and quality of life of the physical, fiscal and social kind, of the more enduring nature at the human level, is entirely about this question of ageing well.

Another common theme in this volume is that of innovation. Harding speaks of innovating — to help seniors age-in-place — to form collaborative projects among different stakeholders in order to achieve shared goals. Innovation is needed to enhance the scientific and technological bases on which we prepare ourselves for the future; for re-conceptualising life, liveability, economic activity, community, and the whole point of development.

This brings us back to Chapter 13 where the Maker Mindset that Veerappan introduces us to has precisely that impulse of invention and innovation but at the popular level. This is much like the National Parks Board with its initiatives to enhance the laypersons' ability to contribute his or her part to the sustainability of the city-state. This involvement or public engagement is ultimately the way in which everyone can adopt a sustainability mindset which is lofty but also practical. The various programmes that his outfit, Ground-Up Initiative presents, pulls together all three pillars of development.

This is what Leong says is the weak link in Singapore's development story — more than not, people have yet to appreciate nature and the environment for its own sake; they lack the appreciation and the sense of agency.

Throughout this volume, we read of a Singapore where the government gets it right; and businesses do what they must within how the government gets it right. Veerappan, Er and Soh, Geh and Harding provide us with the counterpoint that Singaporeans can and do have the right impulses about sustainability; they simply need more platforms, the space and licence now to go on to innovate, at their level and in civic movements to complement the actions of the state.

We hope this Introduction suggests how these essays are still relevant to the policy and governance challenges of the present time in Singapore. The fourth generation of leaders led by current Deputy Prime Minister Lawrence Wong launched the "Forward Singapore" movement that reminds one of the close nexus among the people, the economy and the environment. This volume provides inspiration for innovation and solutions where fresh and significant efforts are needed ground up to form a critical mass of energy of the social and certainly renewable kind. We are grateful to the intellectuals whose works are reproduced here for investing in a better future for Singapore and its people through their thought-leadership over the years.

# Economy

# Chapter 1

# Singapore's Economic Development, 1965–2020: Review, Reflection and Perspective*

*Tan Khee Giap, Evan Tan Beng Kai and Vincent Kwan Wen Seng*

*This article was originally published in Commentary, Volume 24 titled "Singapore@50: Reflections and Observations" © 2015 The National University of Singapore Society. Dr Tan Khee Giap is the Chairman, Singapore National Committee for Pacific Economic Cooperation. At the time of writing, Dr Tan was the Co-Director at the Asia Competitiveness Institute, Lee Kuan Yew School of Public Policy, National University of Singapore. Evan Tan Beng Kai and Vincent Kwan Wen Seng were research assistants at the same institute.

## Introduction

To review the past is not just to retain our harsh memory, but more importantly, it is to better understand how far Singapore has travelled and been transformed in the process of nation-building through the long and uncertain road of fear and anxiety into the cosmopolitan city-state that it is today. Only through a better appreciation of the past efforts of Singapore's founding leaders and contributions by the pioneer generation of Singaporeans, can we continue to move forward with resilience and optimism.

To provide a broad background for contrast, it is useful to compare the growth of the economy or gross domestic product (GDP) and the level of GDP per capita achieved by Singapore, Hong Kong and Malaysia. It is interesting to compare the achievements of Singapore to Malaysia given how these two countries went their separate ways five decades ago, while benchmarking Singapore against Hong Kong is always relevant as both these city-states are of the same population size, but are very different in terms of socio-political economy.

As seen in Figure 1, GDP of Hong Kong began to surge ahead of Singapore and Malaysia after the mid-1970s with aggressive expansion of the economy occurring through the 1980s and beyond 2000. This was fueled mainly by the robust growth of the Chinese economy especially after its accession to the World Trade Organisation in 2002. The growth slowed in 2008 and was sharply overtaken by Singapore and Malaysia from 2009 onwards, which were not as badly affected by the global financial tsunami that broke out at that time.

Notwithstanding the fact that Malaysia is well-endowed with natural resources including plantation crops, commodities for export, natural gas, as well as a relative bigger domestic market because of its much larger population base, Singapore has been able to closely track the size of the Malaysian economy throughout the last five decades. This, in spite of the great handicaps Singapore faced in terms of poor natural endowment, a smaller population and domestic market size. However, the GDP gap

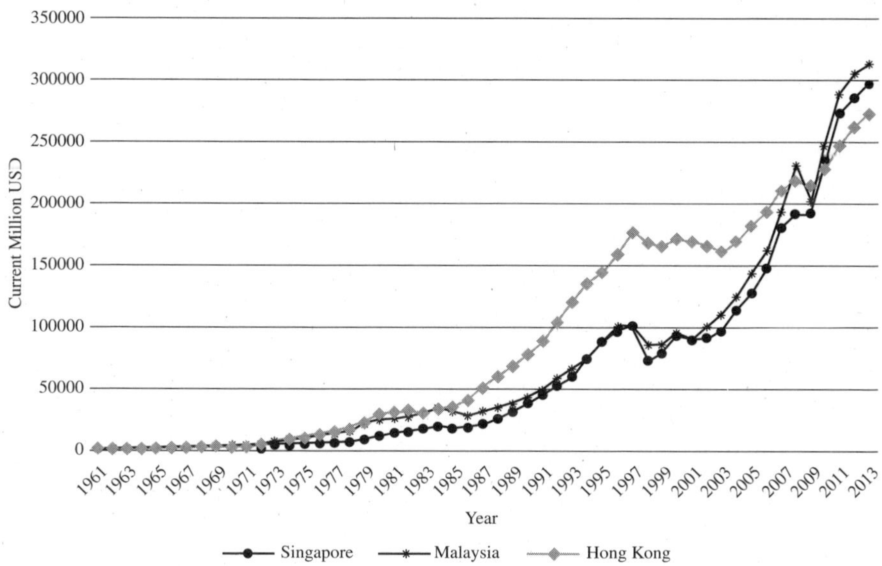


**Figure 1:** Nominal GDP for Singapore Malaysia and Hong Kong, 1961–2013

*Data Source*: The World Bank, World Development Indicators, http://data.worldbank.org/country, 2015

between them began to widen from 2011. Singapore's infrastructural bottleneck, manpower capacity constraint and domestic political pressure for a slower pace of economic growth may further restrict business and economic activities.

As summarised in Figure 2, in terms of GDP per capita, Singapore was tracking closely with Hong Kong throughout the 1970s and 1980s, before it dipped marginally below Hong Kong after the Asian Financial Crisis which broke out in 1997 but then recovered robustly to overtake Hong Kong with a widening margin since 2004, partly propelled by a stronger and appreciating Singapore dollar while the Hong Kong dollar remained pegged to the greenback from 1984.

By 2013, nominal GDP per capita for Singapore with a population of 5.6 million stood at US$55,182 while Hong Kong registered at US$38,123 with a population of 7.8 million, a substantial 30 percent lower. Rather more worrisome for Malaysia, a nation

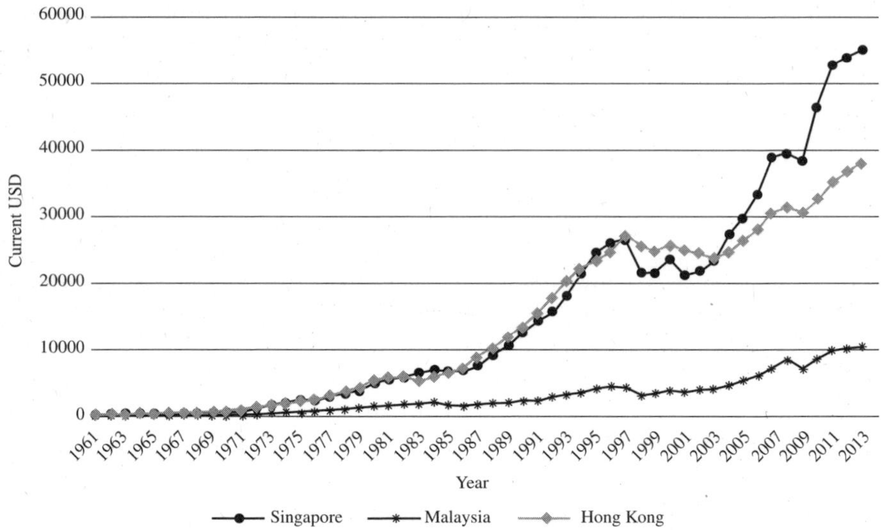


**Figure 2:** Nominal GDP Per Capita for Singapore, Malaysia and Hong Kong, 1961–2013

*Data Source*: The World Bank, World Development Indicators, http://data.worldbank.org/country, 2015

of 28 million people, her GDP per capita dipped slightly in 1997 and has remained trapped at around the US$10,000 level since 2010.

In comparing and contrasting Singapore's economic performance with that of Malaysia and Hong Kong, we will delve in greater detail into the essence of Singapore's economic growth strategies and in particular, the role of its Government. We will address some of the problems Singapore encountered, identify issues pertaining to the challenging economic restructuring that is underway, and the implications related to the potential GDP path ahead.

## Reviewing Economic Development after the Exit from Malaysia

Exactly five decades ago, Singapore became a country rather unexpectedly on 9 August 1965 with no outpouring of triumph or jubilation accompanying it. It was with shock and reluctance that Singapore took on the uphill task of nation-building as a resource-poor island-state with no economic hinterland, exacerbated by hostile relations with neighbouring economies, including Malaysia and Indonesia, as well as domestic political and social unrest.

A serious racial riot exploded in July 1964, which led to the declaration of curfew. Another race riot took place in July 1965. The social fabric of this island-state characterised as being multiethnic, multireligious and multilanguage was torn apart. The period of "Confrontation" broke out with neighbouring Indonesia and only ended after a peace agreement was signed in August 1966. This had disrupted economic development somewhat. Street rioting by leftwing activists throughout the 1960s caused tremendous tension amongst the multiracial community. Singapore's longer-term stability was seriously threatened.

To many citizens then, including the political leadership on both sides of the Causeway, Singapore had neither the necessary attributes nor sufficient conditions to become a viable nation. In fact, there was a time when many people doubted Singapore could ever make it, but we did and the rest is history. Today, the Republic of Singapore is a highly liveable and economically viable cosmopolitan city-state, enjoying the highest degree of racial harmony, sound industrial relations and social stability as measurable by any international yardstick. This should not be taken for granted.

The cornerstone of Singapore's success lies in the facilitative role of its Government with pragmatic public policy formulation implement through a proactive and lean civil service system and zero tolerance for corruption. In a relatively short period of time, an impressive 85 percent ownership of public housing by the populace was achieved under the innovative co-payment Central Provident Fund (CPF) scheme with contributions by both employers and employees, sparing the Government the need for a lumbering state welfare system.

Given the lack of natural resources, Singapore had few options other than to undertake long-term investment in its people through education by establishing high quality schools, tertiary institutions and universities. Through the work of the Economic Development Board (EDB), Singapore aggressively solicited, grew, and retained foreign direct investment from multinational corporations (MNCs), but native skills were rapidly becoming obsolete and unable to match the modern skill sets required by new jobs. This was where the education system was central to the development process.

Over the decades, the Republic has gradually and consistently built up a comprehensive physical infrastructure network with roads, expressways and the mass rapid transit (MRT) system, integrating these with sustainable and environmentally-conscious practices. In retrospect, infrastructure development and investment should have been ramped up by several notches to cope with greater demands from a rapid growth in population, but prudent consideration prevailed in light of the uncertain nature of economic performance. The balance had to be struck between ensuring sustainable and efficient use of government revenues versus increasingly onerous government expenditures incurred. Preparation for a rapidly ageing population with longer life spans, due to years of good healthcare services, has become the new imperative.

Given its limited land mass, Singapore became one of the most densely-populated cities globally in 2013, with total population reaching 5.6 million. In order to grow and achieve the critical mass effect, Singapore embarked upon the external wing policy in the early 1990s with International Enterprise (IE) designed to help Singapore companies venture abroad to overcome the limited domestic market size. Singapore has thus successfully plugged herself into the global trading networks with international trade and services now amounting to three times the size of her GDP. Singapore is now an highly efficient regional hub for financial, aviation, maritime, logistics and telecommunication activities.

After decades of prudent government budgeting and the establishment of professional investment vehicles such as the Government Investment Corporation and Temasek Holdings to manage government surpluses, Singapore has accumulated ample financial resources that can be called upon to deal with future challenges and potential long-drawn-out external shocks, so long as we think rationally as a group and behave with responsibility as one united people within a pluralistic society.

When Singapore left Malaysia in 1965, her nominal GDP was at US$0.97 billion as compared to Malaysia's US$3.2 billion, less than a third of Malaysia's economy. Singapore's economy quickly expanded to half of Malaysia's GDP size in 1977 and reached nearly 69 percent by 1987 and continued to expand to reach the size of Malaysia's GDP by 1997, as both economies propelled forward at around 9 percent growth per annum between 1987 and 1997. Singapore, being a highly open export-oriented economy, was more vulnerable to external shocks, and the size of its economy has hovered around 95 percent of Malaysia between 2007 and 2013 as shown in Table 1.

Singapore started as a multiethnic society of immigrants. Being a poor and new nation, improving standards of living through job creation and public housing provision within a harmonious social setting were the immediate tasks of the Government, which was still going through intense struggles with the left-wing political movement. Since ethnic Chinese-Singaporeans constituted of a large proportion of the population, the Chinese merchants played a leading role in the community and provided a strong economic foundation and stable social environment crucial to Singapore's economic success.

President Tony Tan Keng Yam said at the Singapore Chinese Chamber of Commerce & Industry SG50 Outstanding Chinese Business Pioneer Awards on 6 February 2015 at the Ritz Carlton Hotel, Singapore, "The pioneer generation of Chinese entrepreneurs demonstrated great fortitude in the face of many difficulties in the early years of Singapore's growth journey. As the Singapore economy evolved and progressed, these business pioneers seized opportunities and adapted to the environment. Our pioneers believed in Singapore's future and remained rooted here. Apart from succeeding in their respective fields, many of these pioneers also made it a point to give back to society."[1]

[1] Tan, Tony Keng Yam, speech at the Singapore Chinese Chamber of Commerce & Industry SG50 Outstanding Chinese Business Pioneer Awards, Ritz Carlton Hotel, Singapore, February 6, 2015.

**Table 1:** Major macroeconomic indicators for Singapore and Malaysia, 1987–2013
Singapore & Malaysia: GDP growth*, unemployment rate, inflation & Gini coefficient

| Fiscal Year | Real GDP Growth/ Gini Coefficient | | Unemployment Rate | | Composite CPI Growth | |
|---|---|---|---|---|---|---|
| | **Malaysia** | **Singapore** | **Malaysia** | **Singapore** | **Malaysia** | **Singapore** |
| 1998 | –7.4% | –2.2% | 3.2% | 2.5% | 5.3% | –0.3% |
| 1999 | 6.1% | 6.1% | 3.4% | 2.8% | 2.7% | 0% |
| 2000 | 8.9% | 8.9% | 3.0% | 2.7% | 1.5% | 1.4% |
| 2001 | 0.5% (0.46) | –0.9% (0.45) | 3.5% | 2.7% | 1.4% | 1.0% |
| 2002 | 5.4% | 4.2% | 3.5% | 3.6% | 1.8% | –0.4% |
| 2003 | 5.8% | 4.4% | 3.6% | 4.0% | 1.0% | 0.5% |
| 2004 | 6.8% | 9.5% | 3.5% | 3.4% | 1.5% | 1.7% |
| 2005 | 5.3% | 7.5% | 3.5% | 3.1% | 3.0% | 0.4% |
| 2006 | 5.6% (0.46) | 8.7% (0.47) | 3.3% | 2.7% | 3.6% | 1.0% |
| 2007 | 6.3% | 9.1% | 3.2% | 2.1% | 2.0% | 2.1% |
| 2008 | 4.8% | 1.8% | 3.3% | 2.2% | 5.4% | 6.5% |
| 2009 | –1.5% | –0.6% | 3.7% | 3.0% | 0.6% | 0.6% |
| 2010 | 7.4% (0.44) | 15.2% (0.47) | 3.4% | 2.2% | 1.7% | 2.8% |

| GDP | 1977–1997 | 1998–2008 |
|---|---|---|
| Growth | 8.9% p.a. | 4.4% p.a. |
| Malaysia | 9.2% p.a. | 5.2% p.a. |
| Singapore | | |

| GDP Size | 1977/1987 | 1997 | 2007 | 2013 |
|---|---|---|---|---|
| Malaysia | US$14/32 billion | US$100 billion | US$194 billion | US$313 billion |
| Singapore | US$7/22 billion | US$100 billion | US$180 billion | US$298 billion |
| (SNG/MAL) | 50%/69% | 100% | 93% | 95% |

*Data Source*: The World Bank, http://data.worldbank.org/indicator, 2015

Department of Statistics Singapore, "Table 14: Gini coefficient Among Resident Employed Households, 2000–2013", 2014

Department of Statistics Malaysia, Household Income and Basic Amenities Survey Report 2009, 2012

Department of Statistics Malaysia, Household Income and Basic Amenities Survey Report 2012, 2013

*Note*: *2000–2020 Potential GDP Growth Rate: Malaysia: 5.5%; Singapore: 4.5% (projected by ACI at LKYSPP, NUS); 2013 Per Capita GDP: Singapore US$55,182; Malaysia US$10,538

In fact, we should pay tribute to the broader business community, especially the small and medium enterprises (SMEs) that provided crucial social stability to the society in terms of employment, exemplary work ethic and entrepreneurship. At times of economic restructuring, the Government then tried very hard to attract MNCs to create jobs and acquired global corporate management skills for Singaporeans. The Singapore business community, including big and small companies, contributed to Singapore's national defence plan and in promoting education, helped create a competitive economy, strong security in defence, and preserved the value of traditional culture and harmonious racial relations.

According to projections by Asia Competitiveness Institute (ACI) at the Lee Kuan Yew School of Public Policy (LKYSPP), National University of Singapore (NUS), potential GDP growth per annum for Singapore and Malaysia may be 4.5 percent and 5.5 percent respectively for the period from 2000 to 2020. The former appears to have grown above its potential level whereas the latter grew considerably below its potential output over the period of 1998 to 2008. Price stability prevailed in both countries from 1998 to 2010, as inflation registered at 1.3 percent for Singapore although this was higher at 2.4 percent for Malaysia. Correspondingly over the same period, Singapore managed to achieve fairly low unemployment rate averaging at 2.9 percent as compared to a higher rate of 3.4 percent for Malaysia. As for income disparity measured by the Gini coefficient, it was around 0.46 for Singapore and Malaysia from 2000 onwards. Both countries could have done better on this count.

Based on the annual economic competitiveness ranking conducted by ACI at LKYSPP which tracked ASEAN-10 economies from 2000 onwards, Singapore consistently ranked in the top position, followed by Malaysia. As revealed by the standardised score, the former at 2.0507 means it was at least twice as competitive as the latter, calculated to be at 1.0601.[2]

---

[2] Tan, Khee Giap, Low, Linda, Tan, Kong Yam, and Lim, Lijuan, *Annual Analysis of Competitiveness, Development Strategies and Public Policies on ASEAN-10: 2000–2010* (Singapore: Pearson Education South Asia Pte. Ltd, 2013); Tan, Khee Giap, and Tan, Kong Yam "Assessing Competitiveness of ASEAN-10 Economies," *International Journal of Economics and Business Research* 8, no. 4 (2014), 377–398.

We thus conjecture that such superior relative economic competitive advantage enjoyed by Singapore over Malaysia can be traced to differences in policy formulation and implementation. There exists in the latter government inefficiencies, a lack of adequate governance and the presence of policies to favour "sons of soil" or *bumiputra* as it is referred to in the Malay language, which have been broadly implemented in fields including business, education, housing and land policies. Furthermore, as Malaysia moved into a two-party system more than a decade ago, precious effort and time have been diverted to long-drawn public policy debates, political conflicts and social confrontation at the expense of formulating longer-term economic growth strategies and realising key policy objectives.

## Singapore's Economic Takeoff and Transformation into a Cosmopolitan City

To fully appreciate Singapore's economic growth model, we have to look at the growth strategies at different phases of transformation over the past five decades. Between 1965 and 1986, Singapore experienced an average GDP growth of 8.6 percent per annum under the labour-intensive production-driven phase where the primary objective was employment creation. Between 1987 and 1997, the republic registered an average GDP growth of 9.3 percent per annum under the capital-intensive investment-driven phase where the objective was to upgrade the quality of economic growth through labour-saving strategy.

Between 1998 and 2008, Singapore went through a much lower average GDP growth of 5.2 percent per annum under the innovation-based, technology-driven phase as the city-state attempted to move up the technological ladder. By 2009 and beyond, as regional competitiveness intensified and business costs started to hike, Singapore entered into the productivity-enhancement value-added-driven phase where the economy is currently facing some adjustment difficulties, especially in the business services and construction sectors, which have become used to an abundant supply of relatively cheaper foreign labour.

Currently, the densely populated cosmopolitan island-state is facing a twin policy dilemma with some hard choices to make. On one hand, it is about the desirable magnitude of economic growth, which would have a direct bearing on the level of wage growth and labour productivity growth. On the other hand, the public must also decide on a socially tolerable and politically acceptable foreign workforce pool, which would impact on business costs and economic activities. Thus, this section of the chapter sharpens the focus on the trade-offs involved in Singapore's economic growth strategies looking ahead.

Firstly, has Singapore's economy expanded too fast? Would problems such as income disparity, rising housing prices, public transportation and traffic congestion have been avoided if growth was merely moderate? Secondly, can the Government significantly mitigate these problems through fundamental changes in public policies even as Singapore strives to be more inclusive? Thirdly, as public discontent escalates between the haves and have-nots, can income disparity be significantly mitigated to prevent the emergence of an economic underclass without resorting to a comprehensive social welfare system, which will not only be a financial burden on the state but a disincentive to taxpayers and businesses. This is especially pertinent as Singapore's population ages.

As illustrated in Figure 3, in the period of 1998 to 2008, Singapore went through four externally-driven economic crises and yet managed to achieve an average of GDP growth of 5.2 percent per annum. These were the 1998 recession caused by the 1997 Asian Financial Crisis, the bursting of the American "dot.com" bubble in 2001, and the outbreak of the Severely Acute Respiratory Syndrome (SARS) in 2003. Singapore's economy contracted again in 2009 due to the global financial tsunami of the sub-prime crisis in the United States (US).

Note that between 1987 and 1997, when the external environment was still favourable, Singapore went through robust annual GDP growth of 9.2 percent. As with all maturing economies, it is an enviable growth rate that is unlikely to be repeated. Interestingly, in those years, not many in Singapore complained that the growth was too high or too fast, as the economic gains were more evenly distributed and the public was less outspoken.

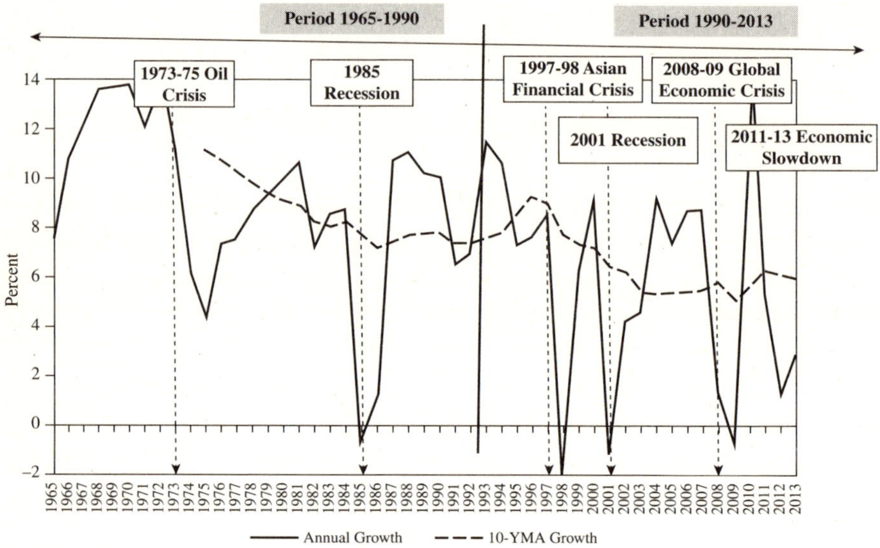


**Figure 3:** Singapore GDP Growth cycles and trends, 1965–2013

*Data Source*: The World Bank, http://data.worldbank.org/indicator, 2015

## Did the Singapore Economy Grow Too High and Too Fast and Can We Optimally Chart Our Own Growth Path?

According to the 2013 data from the International Monetary Fund, Singaporeans were the third wealthiest people in the world in terms of per capita GDP, after Qatar and Luxembourg. However, such rankings are not meaningful if we also recognise Singapore to be perhaps the world's most vulnerable open economy with trade being three times the size of her GDP. When the 2009 American sub-prime crisis kicked in, Singapore was amongst the first to tail-spin into a recession, forcing the Government to dip into its coffers and National Reserves to ease the effects of the economic downturn for companies and minimise the level of unemployment by deploying the Jobs Credit Scheme.

Given the slow recovery of the US economy, notwithstanding quantitative easing by the European Central Bank announced to begin by March 2015, the external debt-driven fiscal weakness will continue to ferment within the European Union (EU). The economic crisis plaguing European economies are unlikely to be quickly resolved as they reflect deep-seated structural problems of eroding competitiveness and the heavy burden of the welfare system. As two major export markets for Singapore, the US and EU were the sources of external shocks to the Singapore economy.

In our recent research on "Asia's Drivers of Growth", we concluded that given existing trade linkages, the US and the EU are still amongst the major engines of growth for all Asian economies, except Taiwan and Hong Kong.[3] As western economies get the chills, Singapore will be the first to catch a severe cold even if we exercise regularly and have antibiotics on standby! We therefore cannot be immune from troubles of these developed western regions.

Singapore went through a drastic economic slowdown in 2012 soon after the US subprime-led recession in 2009. It will become more expensive to finance the European sovereign debts with deteriorating international confidence as the required painful austerity measures continue to be resisted by the European public at large. In the face of such headwinds, no amount of support even with the Jobs Credit Scheme could have averted the rapid economic slowdown in 2012 for Singapore because as a small and highly open economy, we can only strive to be better prepared and deal effectively with exogenous shocks over which we have very limited control.

Amongst the most misunderstood grievance the public has raised is that the Singapore economy has grown too fast and at all cost. Such arguments inappropriately assume that the Government can easily control and decide the speed and magnitude of GDP growth, accelerating or decelerating the economy as desired.

Even if it were true, it does not make logical sense that when the external environment is highly favourable, the Government should curtail employment growth by tightening the labour market, driving

---

[3] Tan, Kong Yam, Tilak, Abeysinghe, and Tan, Khee Giap, "Shifting Drivers of Growth: Policy Implications for ASEAN-5," *Asian Economic Papers* 14, no. 1 (2014).

up business costs in a bid to slow economic growth. Such a direct interventionist approach would have serious repercussions on businesses and potential investors. Should multinationals conclude that such government measures to be the official mode of economic management and make a decision to shift their investment plans elsewhere, it would be most unlikely to see them relocate to Singapore.

## Strategies and Policy Trade-Off Going Forward: Can We Have Our Cake and Eat It Too?

Thus, it is unwise for the Government to impede robust economic growth in good times through curtailing employment growth in response to public resistance to the presence of a large foreign workforce or being pressured by other social-political considerations. Such populist approaches could spell trouble for the Government of the day du jour. It is unrealistic to expect the Government to dip into its funds regularly for special transfers or to be able to sustain balanced budgets for the full term of the elected government should the future be riddled by a higher frequency of recessions, propelled by circumstances outside of Singapore's control.

During the period between 1998 and 2008, economic growth averaged 5.2 percent and this masked the volatility brought on by recessions that were followed by near double-digit growth rates. Over this period, Singapore actually achieved annual employment growth of 2.9 percent and annual average productivity growth of 2.5 percent. This performance was merely a third of the annual growth rate of 9.3 percent for the period between 1987 to 1997.

The question at hand, then, is not whether Singapore's GDP has expanded too fast or if the authorities have pursued growth at all costs. Regardless of growth quantum, it falls upon those in the Government to muster better plans and coordinate government agencies to respond to anticipated infrastructure demand; identify and understand the types of jobs being generated, along with ensuring that the local workforce has the requisite skill sets to take them; forecast public housing needed, make provision for affordable and accessible healthcare and maintain a sustainable living environment in support of a bigger population. In fact, we would venture to argue that even if average GDP growth were to be only half of the period of 1998 to 2008, many of these aforementioned problems might continue to prevail rather than diminish amidst growing budgetary constraints.

It would be a misdirection of criticism to blame the Government for seizing robust economic growth when the external environment permits. It is precisely the adoption of such pro-growth strategy which ensured that Singapore had the resources to maintain fiscal sustainability and prudence over the ups and downs of business cycles. It is timely however to redefine the fundamental philosophy underpinning our economic policies to incorporate the need for the Government to facilitate greater social inclusion even as it seeks to take advantage of the opportunities presented by the external environment.

To rephrase the issues and questions at hand again for serious consideration: Should the Government cave in to populist political demands by artificially and abruptly choking off the flow of essential foreign labour supply required for business expansion and hence, slow down economic and wage growth, or should we deploy greater effort and government surpluses to sharpen the ability of Singaporean worker to compete by raising the skills and productivity of workers especially among those who have fallen behind?

## Rapid Globalisation: Economic Restructuring and Issues Encountered

Singapore has taken full advantage of the globalisation process by plugging herself into a global trading network, pioneering free trade agreements (FTAs), facilitated by its rising stature as an international financial centre as well as an efficient international aviation and maritime hub. As much as Singapore has reaped the benefits of globalisation through trade and finance, with it were unwelcomed side effects of widening income disparity, rising housing prices and an overcrowded public transport system.

However, as Singapore moves up the technological ladder with intensified regional competition coming from neighbouring ASEAN countries as well as China and India, skill sets possessed by Singaporeans born in the 1950s and 1960s are fast becoming irrelevant to higher value-added jobs now available. Attempts to boost productivity have not yielded the results needed to match the demand of a rapidly restructuring economy. Singaporeans from low-income households that received only secondary level or lower-education, are increasingly trapped in an economic underclass, and further disadvantaged by factors such as larger family sizes and deficits in social capital and the quality of their information networks.

Singapore's income disparity as measured by the Gini coefficient has rapidly worsened since the late 1990s registering its worst reading of 0.48 in 2012.

With the quickening pace of globalisation, heavy subsidies for education, healthcare, public utilities and CPF top-ups were made available through special transfers from the annual budget which came to $2.6 billion per year from 2000 to 2009. According to computation by Department of Statistics in 2013, such special transfers were able to contain the Gini coefficient at around 0.44, the same level as in 2000.

Over the same period, we have observed a widening gap in the growth of income for the highest 20 percentile households versus the lowest 20 percentile households. It behooves economists to examine why the income gap is widening — the thesis that globalisation and technological advances are rendering lowly trained skills obsolete may not offer a comprehensive account of the widening gap.

## Benchmarking Economic Performances of Two City-States: Hong Kong versus Singapore

Singapore is not as fortunate as Hong Kong, which was able to and is still benefitting from the Mainland and Hong Kong Closer Economic Partnership Arrangement (CEPA) as well as World

Trade Organisation (WTO) Plus concessions, with China rapidly expanding as an economic powerhouse. While Hong Kong's defence is entirely taken care of by the People's Liberation Army (PLA) of her motherland, Singapore reserves a substantial portion of her annual budget to maintain her defence capabilities. More than occasional friction with neighbouring countries distract from what would have otherwise been even closer economic cooperation within ASEAN.

In comparison, Hong Kong's GDP grew at an annual rate of 6 percent in the 1987 to 1997 period and 3.8 percent in the 1998 to 2008 period, about 40 percent lower than what Singapore achieved over the same period. Interestingly, when we contrasted the performance of the two city-states, we found that whenever there was a recession, Hong Kong would sink deeper, and whenever the economy recovered, Singapore would rebound higher. In comparison, Singapore's GDP was only 43 percent that of Hong Kong's between 1977 and 1987, before it quickly caught up to 56 percent and 85 percent in 1997 and 2007 respectively and has since surpassed Hong Kong by 9 percent in 2013.

One may conclude that the positive interventionist approach has enabled the Singapore Government to squeeze relatively more growth from the economy than the non-interventionist Hong Kong authorities. Furthermore, Hong Kong's economy was constrained by the rigid Hong Kong-US dollar exchange rate peg regime that prevented the economy from making cost adjustments through exchange rate movements, which necessitates deep price corrections in the stock market and risks severe downturn in the real-estate sector.

The Hong Kong Government's Long Term Fiscal Planning Working Group pointed out in 2014 that "if Hong Kong government still insists on all kinds of public service expenditures and based on the present trend, structural government budget deficit is projected to prevail in seven years' time (2021), and all government surpluses will be used up by 2028, thereafter would have to resort to borrowing". This is the fiscal predicament of Hong Kong after having built up a comprehensive and expensive welfare system that Singapore must not indulge in.

**Table 2:** Major macroeconomic indicators for Singapore and Hong Kong, 1998–2013 Singapore & Hong Kong: GDP growth*, unemployment rate, inflation & Gini coeff.

| Fiscal | Real GDP Growth/Gini Coefficient | | Unemployment Rate | | Composite CPI Growth | |
|---|---|---|---|---|---|---|
| Year | Hong Kong | Singapore | Hong Kong | Singapore | Hong Kong | Singapore |
| 1998 | –5.9% | –2.2% | 2.2% | 2.5% | 2.9% | –0.3% |
| 1999 | 2.5% | 6.1% | 4.6% | 2.8% | –4.0% | 0% |
| 2000 | 7.7% | 8.9% | 6.2% | 2.7% | –3.7% | 1.4% |
| 2001 | 0.5% (0.53) | –0.9% (0.45) | 4.9% | 2.7% | –1.7% | 1.0% |
| 2002 | 1.7% | 4.2% | 5.1% | 3.6% | –3.1% | –0.4% |
| 2003 | 3.1% | 4.4% | 7.3% | 4.0% | –2.5% | 0.5% |
| 2004 | 8.7% | 9.5% | 7.9% | 3.4% | –0.4% | 1.7% |
| 2005 | 7.4% | 7.5% | 6.7% | 3.1% | 0.9% | 0.4% |
| 2006 | 7.0% (0.53) | 8.7% (0.47) | 5.6% | 2.7% | 2.1% | 1.0% |
| 2007 | 6.5% | 9.1% | 4.8% | 2.1% | 2.0% | 2.1% |
| 2008 | 2.1% | 1.8% | 4.0% | 2.2% | 4.3% | 6.5% |
| 2009 | –2.5% | –0.6% | 3.6% | 3.0% | 0.6% | 0.6% |
| 2010 | 6.8% (0.53) | 15.2% (0.47) | 5.2% | 2.2% | 2.3% | 2.8% |

| GDP Growth | 1977–1997 | 1998–2008 |
|---|---|---|
| Hong Kong | 6.0% p.a. | 3.8% p.a. |
| Singapore | 9.2% p.a. | 5.2% p.a. |

| GDP Size | 1977/1987 | 1997 | 2007 | 2013 |
|---|---|---|---|---|
| Hong Kong | US$16/51 billion | US$177 billion | US$212 billion | US$274 billion |
| Singapore | US$7/22 billion | US$100 billion | US$180 billion | US$298 billion |
| (SNG/HK) | 43%/43% | 56% | 85% | 109% |

*Data Source*: The World Bank, http://data.worldbank.org/indicator, 2015

Department of Statistics Singapore, "Table 14: Gini coefficient Among Resident Employed Households, 2000–2013", 2014

Hong Kong Census and Statistics Department, 2006 Population Census — Thematic Report: Household Income Distribution in Hong Kong, 2007

Hong Kong Census and Statistics Department, 2011 Population Census — Thematic Report: Household Income Distribution in Hong Kong, 2012

*Note*: *2000–2020 Potential GDP Growth Rate: Hong Kong: 3.5%; Singapore: 4.5% (Projected by ACI at LKYSPP, NUS); 2013 Per Capita GDP: Singapore US$55,182; Hong Kong US$38,123

In contrast, the Singapore Government has been under pressure to cater for large demand for special transfers or subsidies in each annual government budget to mitigate income disparity and the effect of an ageing population. In fact, the special transfers from the annual budget have doubled since 2009, and are expected to remain at the same level if not rise in the future.

## Overcoming Public Expectations and External Challenges: Reflection and Perspective

After the robust GDP growth of 15 percent for 2010 from 1 percent contraction in 2009, Singapore has registered GDP growth at an average rate of 3.3 percent per annum between 2011 and 2014 that is lower than the potential rate of 4.5 percent per annum estimated by ACI. The lower growth performance was mainly due to labour supply adjustments by the Government to improve productivity coupled with pressure from the public to scale down on foreign workforce engagement. Companies with orders were therefore not able to expand their business activities, with some companies considering relocation which could pose a big risk to Singapore. This is a policy area Singapore needs to calibrate and tread very carefully into.

Singapore has, in the past, been ranked by international agencies to be among the world's top five positions for 2013 in terms of being the freest economy, least risky for investment, least corrupt and the most competitive economy overall.

Over the business cycles, successive terms of pro-active governments were able to achieve above-potential GDP growth for nearly five decades and a healthy budgetary position. This was due to political stability and racial harmony, coupled with its relentless effort to diversify the economy. Nevertheless, such a growth strategy, began to be questioned in certain quarters and culminated in the dissatisfaction as expressed in popular votes at the General Election (GE) of 2011.

## An Inclusive Society: Public Housing Policy and Harmonious Industrial Relations

Addressing income disparity and building an inclusive society is a national commitment, but consensus is required to determine how to go about achieving it. Pertinent questions include what the basic principles for growing that inclusivity are, how costly and sustainable would it be, how is such an inclusive society is funded and who would be paying for it.

Public housing is an important social equaliser, a unique facet of Singapore's way of life and an integral part of the asset enhancement programme within a land-scarce, rapidly growing city-state. Home ownership would be meaningless if the value of the property does not appreciate or worse, stagnates or depreciates over time. Discounted prices and incentives are therefore necessary for first time home-buyers. Discussion as to how the Government can ensure the fruits of the land and asset property appreciation are to be fairly distributed to those citizens and are prepared to work for it, holds the key to developing a fresh consensus around achieving that sense of inclusion in Singapore.

Effective tripartite relationships amongst the workers, employers and the Government must remain the cornerstone of Singapore's harmonious industrial relations. These have allowed Singapore to achieve economic competitiveness, high productivity and employment stability.

## Subsidising Public Services and Tracking of Four Essential Affordability Indices

Provision of public services including education, healthcare, public housing and public transportation constitute a significant portion of the cost of living for average citizens. Should such essential services be privatised or nationalised? After GE2011, the Singapore Government has quite rightly abandoned the breakeven cost-recovery market pricing (BCMP) strategy for public services, moving away from the past ultra-prudent budgetary principle.

Such policy reversals surely cannot come free-of-charge as this would mean bigger government expenditures which would have to be funded in other ways, presumably by tax payers, directly or indirectly. Are you prepared to do so knowing that the burden is likely to grow heavier over time with our rapidly ageing population unless this weight is shared by a younger population through productive new immigrants?

The transparent tracking of affordability would serve to allay public concerns. Periodically disclosed Transparent Affordability Indices (TAIs) may be computed, by working in conjunction with the Government, to assess the affordability of essential public services for average Singaporean residents that can stand up to public scrutiny. This can serve to reinforce public confidence and trust in the Government. Constructing annual international benchmarking indices to compare the world's major cities in terms of cost of living, wages and purchasing power, such as those by ACI in LKYSPP would complement the TAIs.[4]

## Calibrated Steady-State National Manpower Policy: Allocating One-Third Foreign Workforce for the Economy

For continued development and growth, Singapore has no choice but to rely on a large foreign workforce. This is the reality for our city-state, but there is a trade-off involved. To what extent are we prepared to accommodate or tolerate their existence, and how ready would the Government be to meet their needs?

The Government is committed to achieving a steady-state where not more than one-third of the total workforce would be foreigners and ensure that all Singaporeans who want to work would be able to have the skills to find jobs with decent pay through practical educa-

[4] Tan, Khee Giap, Tan, Kong Yam, and Low, Linda, *Annual Indices for Cost of Living, Wages and Purchasing Power for Expatriates and Ordinary Residents in World's Major 103 Cities, 2005–2013* (Singapore: World Scientific Publishing Co. Pte. Ltd, 2015).

tion curriculums, industrial internships, subsidised productivity training and the Workfare Income Supplement (WIS) scheme. Singaporeans should feel confident in the workplace even if they seem to be competing against these foreign workers.

It is therefore paramount for the public to understand and accept that so long as the trend is moving towards the targetted one-third, fluctuation in the foreign workforce hovering above or below this quota would be tolerable over the business cycles. This is to say that whenever the external environment is favourable, we should seize upon external demand to add revenues to the government budget that may have incurred deficits during global economic downturns.

Over the past decade, Singapore was able to create more jobs than the resident workforce could possibly take up. It is therefore crucial for the public to understand and accept that highly skilled white-collar foreign professionals could help to create more jobs. Blue-collar foreign workers are also needed to work on infrastructure projects.

## Quality Employment Creation: Ensuring Two-Third Indigenous PMETs by 2030

As a policy objective, the Government projected that indigenous professionals, managers, executives and technicians (PMETs) would increase from being half of all workers by occupational profile currently to being two-thirds of all workers by 2030, so that we would require relatively less foreign employment pass and S-pass holders by then.

In the event of a protracted low growth economy, either due to companies relocating and/or worsening external demand, would Singapore still be able to create quality jobs for PMETs? Does it make logical sense that when the external environment is highly favourable, the Government should curtail employment growth by tightening labour market conditions so much so that they raise business costs and remove "unwanted" extra business growth, forcing the economy to slow down?

The steady-state projected population of 6.9 million by 2030 is critical in ensuring economic resilience and a consistent growth path for Singapore. The pertinent approach is therefore to attract and retain quality immigrants who can contribute to tax income and who possess the ability to integrate locally.

## Reflections: Stop Being Inward-Looking, Avoid Blind Spots and Pursue Correct Public Policies

Given the ever-rising public expectations, the following are some pertinent questions that Singaporeans should attempt to think through: Are you prepared to see employment creation and business vibrancy in Singapore slow down as MNCs relocate? Would you accept continuing infrastructure bottlenecks and traffic congestion if we do not have enough foreign workers to build them? Would you accept delays in the timelines for building 200,000 units of public housing? Would you be prepared to pay higher taxes in the form of goods and services tax, personnel income tax or corporate profit tax so as to fund higher social spending?

Meanwhile, the Government may want to re-think some of the public policies that served us well in the past but have since gone into auto-pilot which might need recalibration, fine-tuning or even a reverse in direction, although in some cases these reform efforts may have already been taking place.

The HDB may want to consider revamping the affordability index for public housing pricing and rentals in order to appropriately reflect weights assigned according to room-types and income brackets.

The National Environmental Agency may want to look at the cost-of-living index when setting the rental and base-price bidding for hawker stalls to ensure that cooked food for the masses is affordable.

The Public Transport Council may want to reexamine the formula for setting public transportation fares by indexing them to affordability according to capita household income, age groups and inflation.

The Jurong Town Corporation may want to review land costs, factory rentals for small and medium enterprises based on feasibility of business proposals to be judged by an independent private-sector led committee.

The Ministry of Manpower may want to require statutory declaration from human resource directors' that they have actively sourced for local workers to fill job vacancies before approving the applications of foreign workforce for Employment Passes, S Passes and Work Permits.

New inclusive approaches to growth and development would not lead to lower revenues or bigger subsidies for statutory boards, ministries and government-linked companies, but they would instead translate into higher income and employment for Singaporeans. It is certainly superior to implementing a more expensive, fiscally debilitating and comprehensive social safety nets proposed by some quarters.

These inclusive approaches are also more cost effective than the current WIS Scheme, which cannot significantly mitigate income disparity and would continue to be a funding burden with a very remote possibility of these individuals achieving income independence, unless we raise the level of income supplement and link it to upskilling programmes with a graduation timeline imposed.

Using benchmarks gathered over the past decade, ACI at LKYSPP simulated three medium-term GDP growth scenarios achievable under various levels of productivity growth targets, by assuming a certain level of employment, labour share, total factor productivity, labour and capital quality growth.

Based on the actual economic performance of the economy over the period 1998 to 2008, we simulated the associated GDP growth band and productivity target for pessimistic, optimistic and the base case scenarios which we perceived to be most likely for the period 2009 to 2020 as shown in Table 3.

Our base case simulation results suggest that for a policy assumption of 1.5 percent employment growth coupled with other assumptions for capital and labor quality, the Singapore economy would grow at an annual average rate of 4.2 percent

**Table 3:** Simulation of GDP and ALP growth, 2009–2020: Assumptions and projections

| | **Actual 1998–2008** | **Pessimistic Scenario** | **Base Case** | **Optimistic Scenario** | **Remarks** |
|---|---|---|---|---|---|
| Labour share | 0.532 | 0.532^ | 0.532^ | 0.532^ | ^assumed |
| Labour quality growth (%) | 1.24 | 1.00^ | 1.24^ | 1.50^ | ^assumed |
| Capital accumulation enhancement | 0.08 | 0.08^ | 0.25^ | 0.50^ | ^assumed |
| Capital quality growth (%) | 0.29 | 0.18^ | 0.29^ | 0.40^ | ^assumed |
| Total factor productivity growth (%) | 0.51 | 0.30^ | 0.51^ | 0.70^ | ^assumed |
| Employment growth (%) | 2.92 | 1.00 | 1.50 | 2.00 | ^assumed |
| **Productivity growth (%)** | **2.52** | **1.79@** | **2.67@** | **3.61@** | **@projected** |
| **GDP growth (%)** | **5.45** | **2.79@** | **4.17@** | **5.61@** | **@projected** |

*Data Source*: The World Bank, http://data.worldbank.org/indicator, 2015

with required productivity target of 2.7 percent per year for the period 2009 to 2020. Such a GDP growth scenario would mean that Singapore's workforce must be prepared to deliver at the top end of the National Productivity Target (NPT) band of 2 percent to 3 percent as set by the 2009 Economic Strategies Committee (ESC).

For an optimistic scenario, if the authorities should push for an annual average employment growth of 2 percent, the Singapore economy would be able to achieve an average annual GDP growth of 5.6 percent where productivity growth is 3.6 percent. Such a situation would mean achieving the productivity level well above the NPT — a tall order! Such an optimistic scenario implies continued public discontent against the Government as it requires a large foreign workforce, especially during the good years in order to make up for GDP lost during the bad years.

Even as we pursue the base case scenario, the biggest challenge remains as to how the Government could judiciously utilise the budget surpluses generated to mitigate the income disparity through careful calculation and allocation of resources to avoid the emergence of a potential economic underclass. Globalisation and inclusive growth are not mutually exclusive and positive interventionist policies for inclusivity have their place. The challenge for the Government is to prove how income disparity could be addressed by enhancing inclusivity without retreating from globalisation in trade and finance. Being a small and highly open economy with no direct hinterland, Singapore probably does not have many choices.

## Why is Forging National Consensus under a Renewed Social Contract an Imperative?

As Singaporeans become better educated, they are increasingly keen to participate in public policy formulation. However, there is an emerging danger, as it is happening in Taiwan, Hong Kong, Thailand and Malaysia just to name a few countries, where citizens are becoming so inward-looking, totally engrossed in domestic politics and social debate, such that the entire government and bureaucracy are embroiled in conflict and gridlock, draining away precious resources, time and effort.

While all political and cultural debates may ultimately be local, engagement on economic discourse for Singapore should always take the global perspective into consideration. Rational public policies must thus prevail over irrational public pressure. Most of all, public trust towards public institutions and civil servants must not be undermined. Apart from the conventional media and press, the shaping of public opinion and public policy dissemination must be conducted closely with the HDB heartlanders in mind, especially through bi-directional policy feedback channelled from community-based grassroots workers.

Increasing public consultation on government policy is a positive development. However, we consider what type of citizen participation we wish to promote — do we necessarily want a confrontational political process of the two-party system or do we prefer a strong check-and-balance approach by opposition parties on the incumbent government with proven track record, bearing in mind that the choice for the latter model could very well lead back to the first option? Singaporeans will need to give this question careful thought.

# Chapter 2

# Economic and Business Development in Singapore and the World: A Small Economy Perspective*

*David Skilling*

*This article was originally published in Commentary, Volume 27 titled "SGP4.0: An Agenda" © 2018 The National University of Singapore Society. Dr David Skilling is the founding Director of Landfall Strategy Group, a Singapore-based economic advisory firm that provides insights on global economic, political, and policy developments to governments, firms and financial institutions.

Singapore's economic performance has been remarkable over the past several decades, converging rapidly towards the global income frontier. From 30 percent of the per capita income of the United States (US) in 1965, Singapore moved to 110 percent by 1995 and 150 percent in 2017. Singapore sustained average growth rates in its gross domestic product (GDP) of over 5 percent in the decades from the 1970s until the Global Financial Crisis (GFC) a decade ago.

This economic success has been based on a particular economic model — positioning Singapore as a regional and global hub for global firms, talent and capital. As measured by exports and foreign direct investment, Singapore is one of the most open economies in the world. This intense global engagement was supported by strong growth in the labour force, due to its relatively youthful demographic profile then as well as significant migration inflows.

After over 50 years of this strong catch-up growth, however Singapore needs to respond to an emerging series of new challenges (and opportunities). Although GDP growth rates are running at around 4 percent in the first half of 2018, much of the post-crisis growth experienced after the GFC has been muted by Singapore's standards. Looking ahead, the domestic and external environment is likely to be less supportive of Singapore's economic performance.

## A Brave New World?

Several emerging structural dynamics will impact on Singapore's outlook over the next decade and beyond. This discussion considers the structural drivers of slowing GDP growth, the changing external environment, and the impact of disruptive technologies and business models.

### Structural Growth Slowdown

Singapore's trend GDP growth rates have slowed markedly over the past few decades. This is a common pattern across economies as they approach the income frontier. Looking across the current group of advanced economies, GDP growth rates of around 2 to 3 percent on average are common. This gives a baseline for what Singapore can expect. There are fewer "catch-up" opportunities, and economic performance has to come from innovation-led productivity in the Singapore economy.

Reinforcing this structural growth slowdown is weakening growth in Singapore's labour force. Since 2000, about 60 percent of Singapore's headline GDP growth has come from labour force growth and the remaining 40 percent from labour productivity growth.

However, Singapore's labour force will likely grow less rapidly than the average over the past 20 years. The Monetary Authority of Singapore estimates that the proportion of resident working-age population — citizens and permanent residents between the ages of 15 and 64 — to the total will begin to shrink from around 2020. Also, the number of work permits (and other forms of foreign entry into the workforce) has been tightened as an act of conscious economic and social policy. This slowdown is already evident: hours worked and employment contracted in 2017.

As growth rates reduce, the quality of growth becomes more important. Looking around other small advanced economies, many are able to generate strong economic and social outcomes and a dynamic, resilient economy even with growth rates in the 2 percent range. The key is productivity-driven growth.

## A Changing External Environment

Since Independence, Singapore has benefited substantially from a supportive international economic and political environment, that is, intense globalisation undergirded by the rules-based system as well as relative geopolitical stability in the Asian region. Singapore has also been active in positioning itself to benefit from globalisation, signing free trade agreements and engaging actively in regional integration efforts — from the ASEAN Economic Community to the recent Comprehensive and Progressive Agreement for Trans-Pacific Partnership.

But there are deep pressures emerging in the international economic and political system. The "America First" approach of the Trump Administration is sceptical of the international rules-based system, pursuing a more bilateral approach, pulling out of agreements like the original formulation of the Trans-Pacific Partnership, and questioning the value of institutions such as the World Trade Organization. The US has begun to impose tariffs and investment restrictions on China — raising the risk profile around the international trade system.

China's approach to economic policy is also causing stresses in the system, from the nature of market access of foreign firms into China to the industrial policy in the Made in China 2025 Plan. Over the next decade, there is rising potential for consequential trade tension between China and the US.

More broadly, there is growing evidence of a greater intersection between international economic and political relationships. Note, for example, recent Chinese economic pressure on countries such as South Korea and Norway, after bilateral diplomatic tensions. The exemptions granted by the US to recent steel and aluminium tariffs (imposed on national security grounds) were related to the political relationship these countries had with the US.

These tensions are likely to lead to a more fragmented global trade and economic system. Small economies like Singapore are particularly exposed to these dynamics because of their large external sectors as well as their absence of raw political power. Small economies are more comfortable in a rules-based environment. The risk with the emerging environment is that small economies are more likely to be squeezed by larger economic and political powers. It will be a more complex environment for small economies to navigate.

## Disruptive Technologies

A wide range of emerging technologies — such as robotics, autonomous vehicles, 3D printing and the Internet of Things (IoT) — are set to have a disruptive impact on labour markets, firms, and overall economies. Disruptive technological change is not new, but this is now happening at a scale and speed that is unprecedented.

Singapore is well-placed to take advantage of these opportunities as well as to manage the risks. The World Economic Forum (WEF) recently ranked Singapore as one of the best positioned economies to capture value from disruptive technology. Singapore has high levels of human capital and skills, with workers able to upgrade and adapt to new ways of working. This is supported by active government initiatives around skills-upgrading (SkillsFuture as well as through the formal education system).

In addition, the Singapore Government has identified various elements of disruptive technology as a strategic policy priority with an example of this being the Smart Nation Initiative. Singapore is leading with policy and regulatory innovation in areas such as fintech, autonomous vehicles and drones.

These technologies provide a valuable way of pursuing the productivity agenda and compensating for slower labour force growth. Technologies such as automation and the IoT provide ways for firms to strengthen their competitive positions in international markets. Disruptive technologies will also have a meaningful impact on domestic sectors, such as construction and retail. At the same time, these technologies are likely to have a disruptive impact on labour markets, creating and destroying many jobs and changing the nature of occupations for many.

## Learning from Other Small Advanced Economies

These challenges are coming together at the same time to create a more complex environment for policymaking. Although Singapore continues to generate strong outcomes, a determined policy response is needed to adapt to a changing domestic and external context.

In this regard, there is much that Singapore can learn from other small advanced economies, from the Nordics and Switzerland to Ireland and New Zealand. These are small advanced economies that are also operating at the income frontier, have an emphasis on productivity-led growth, acute exposure to the external environment, and a similar set of policy options and constraints as Singapore.

There are many things that can be taken from the international small economy experience, but I would point to three related, mutually-supporting classes of action that can make a meaningful contribution to Singapore.

First, strengthening value capture by building deep clusters in Singapore.

Singapore's economic model is distinguished by the contribution from highly productive foreign firms located in Singapore that have an external focus. However, these activities are not deeply integrated into the Singapore economy itself with their limited local supply chains, increasingly capital intensive activity, and so on. This reduces the amount of value that is captured in the domestic economy from growth in these sectors; the profits flow to overseas shareholders or to a relatively small number of direct employees. This is a challenge also faced by other successful small economies with a heavy reliance on inward foreign direct investment, such as Ireland.

In contrast, other successful small advanced economies have externally-oriented economies that are built on deep, dense clusters of related activity. For example, pharmaceuticals and finance in Switzerland, or maritime and logistics in Denmark. These clusters are based on strong domestic strengths, together with foreign firms and capital, and are surrounded by a supporting ecosystem of research institutes, universities, infrastructure, specialist firms, and so on. These clusters support on-going innovation and productivity, and provide the basis for competitive strength and good jobs even in the context of high cost structures.

In many cases, there will be only a handful of these clusters. Small economies can build critical mass in only a limited number of areas. Singapore needs to focus on building and developing existing Singapore strengths, developing deeply-embedded clusters in the Singapore economy that have greater local content. In short, there should be an effort to transition Singapore over time from a hub for foreign firms to a distinctive platform that supports externally-focused Singapore clusters.

In addition to stronger value capture, this will add to the resilience of Singapore — reducing its exposure to footloose capital. There is a resilience from these embedded clusters because it is hard to replicate these ecosystem characteristics elsewhere. Local firms are likely to be stickier in the country than multinational corporations.

Second, deeper international engagement by Singapore firms in the region.

International engagement is the productivity growth engine of small advanced economies; domestic sectors are too small to generate sustained labour productivity growth rates. Singapore's levels of international engagement are very high even when benchmarked against other small advanced economies, but a significant share of this comes from foreign firms.

At a firm-level, international expansion is critical to the productivity and performance of companies. This is very clear from the international small economy experience. A core part of Singapore's productivity agenda should be focused on supporting the international expansion by Singapore firms. This will require government support. International expansion from a small economy will often come early in a firm's life, involving higher costs and risks. Financial and non-financial support is important to accelerate the process of international expansion.

Singapore's export profile is currently highly diversified across markets — from ASEAN to North Asia, as well as Europe and the US. However, the lesson from other small advanced economies is that regional expansion is very important. For example, over 60 percent of exports from small European economies go to other markets in the European Union (EU).

As global supply chains are unwound — due to both technology and politics — there is likely to be a more regional feel to the global economy. In Asia, this regionalisation of activity will be reinforced by the growing middle class. Even if there are political and economic risks in Asia, Singapore has a privileged position at the centre of

Asia. There are some particular opportunities for Singapore in the region. Singapore's export share to ASEAN has been stable at around 20 percent for the past 15 years and there is headroom for growth.

Third, a greater emphasis on inclusive growth.

Relative to large economies, small advanced economies have combined strong economic performance, high levels of engagement with globalisation, top performance on innovation, together with a range of good social outcomes. For example, small economy Gini coefficients are lower, employment rates are higher, and index measures of overall welfare (from the UN's Human Development Index to the WEF's Inclusive Growth Index) are higher for small advanced economies than for larger economies. Singapore, as a city-state, faces some particular challenges in this regard — although its Gini coefficient is higher than in many other small, advanced economies, it is lower than other global cities such as London, New York, and indeed Hong Kong, that face particular competitive pressures on labour markets. But, despite these constraints, the small economy experience is instructive in pointing to the ways in which economic and social outcomes can be progressed simultaneously.

These outcomes are largely a matter of deliberate policy choice by small advanced economies. Many small advanced economies explicitly combine a commitment to flexible, open markets, comprehensive social insurance, active labour market policy, and high quality education. This has contributed to a compressed income distribution even in the context of globalisation and technological change.

There is an understanding that sustaining support for an economic model that is based on openness to the global economy requires policies to manage the risks. One (persuasive) intuition for this is that the higher levels of social insurance in (small) open economies serve to offset the higher level of volatility in household income that is generated by exposure to external markets. The existence of social insurance, active labour market policy, and lifelong learning education opportunities makes it likely that people will be more willing to take risks — and to be able to respond to adverse events. In a context where disruptive economic and political change is increasingly likely, this characteristic of successful small advanced economies is relevant to Singapore.

This is not just about redistribution, and Singapore should not aim to simply replicate Denmark or Finland. But as the risk profile increases due to globalisation and technology, the design of social insurance should be considered to ensure that risks are allocated efficiently across the economy. The international small economy experience suggests that building an economy driven by innovation and creativity will require progress on these measures.

## Concluding Remarks

The next several years will be a pivotal period for Singapore as key growth drivers markedly slow and new challenges emerge: growth in the country's working age population was essentially zero in 2017; world trade growth has been zero over much of the post-GFC period until recently; risks of a regime change in the global economic system have risen; and a range of disruptive technologies are emerging rapidly.

Singapore is increasingly facing policy issues that are similar to those faced by other small advanced economies. The good news is that other small advanced economies are responding effectively to these challenges and — although local context needs to be taken seriously — Singapore's fourth generation of leaders can learn much from these small economy experiences.

# Chapter 3

# Development of Singapore's Financial Sector*

*Piyush Gupta*

* This article was originally published in Commentary, Volume 24 titled "Singapore @ 50: Reflections and Observations" © 2015 The National University of Singapore Society. Piyush Gupta is Chief Executive Officer and Director of DBS Group, as well as Director of DBS Bank (Hong Kong) Limited and The Islamic Bank of Asia Limited.

In 2012, DBS Bank bid farewell to our long-time home at Shenton Way, and moved to a new headquarters building at Marina Bay Financial Centre (MBFC) Tower 3. Being Singapore's largest bank, our shift to the new premises effectively cemented the MBFC as the country's new financial downtown.

Today, MBFC is a coveted business address, and the Marina Bay area, a vibrant and thriving space that epitomises the cosmopolitan, edgy city that Singapore has become. So, it might defy belief that only 50 years ago, Marina Bay was an open sea.

Marina Bay's transformation, from an open sea to a barren reclaimed land to a financial centre par excellence, is due to the foresight of the Singapore Government. As early as the 1960s, it envisioned the day when the Central Business District (CBD) would need to expand beyond the confines of Shenton Way. Reclamation works were initiated long before Singapore became a regional, global financial centre — long before the need for that piece of real estate existed.

In many ways, the MBFC story is that of Singapore's financial sector development. It is a story of unparalleled success, made possible by bold vision, detailed planning, and a relentless pursuit of excellence.

Singapore is home to over 200 banks today, a growing number of which have chosen to base their operational headquarters here to service their regional group activities. The banking sector has a total asset size of almost US$2 trillion, and employs about 5.5 percent of Singapore's entire workforce of 3.4 million people, or over 180,000 workers.

In 1960, per capita income in Singapore was SG$1,310 (US$428). In 2013, it was SG$69,000, putting the country among the richest in the world. Over the same period, the financial sector's contribution to GDP has risen from 3.9 percent (1960) to about 12 percent today. According to the International Monetary Fund, productivity in Singapore's financial sector has outperformed that in any other financial centre worldwide.

Singapore is also head and shoulder on par with the big boys in the global league. It is a leading wealth management centre, as well as the third-largest foreign exchange centre, behind London and

New York. Singapore is also Asia's leading commodity derivatives trading hub and according to some estimates, accounts for more than half of Asia's over-the-counter (OTC) commodity derivatives trades.

## The Financial Sector Journey

As Founding Prime Minister Lee Kuan Yew wrote in his autobiography *From Third World To First,* "anyone, who predicted in 1965 when we separated from Malaysia that Singapore would become a financial centre, would have been thought mad...It had a most improbable start in 1968."

As the story goes, Albert Winsemius, then an economic advisor for Singapore, wanted to transform Singapore into a financial centre for Southeast Asia within 10 years. In a conversation with a Dutch friend, he was told it could be done in three or four years because Singapore was advantaged by timezone differences. As Winsemius recounted, "He took a globe and showed me a gap in the financial market of the world. Trading, he explained, starts at nine o'clock in the morning in Zurich, Switzerland. An hour later, London opens. When London closes, New York is already open. After closing time on Wall Street, San Francisco on the American west coast is still active — but as soon as San Francisco closes, there is a gap of a few hours. This gap can be filled by Singapore, should the Government not shun taking some drastic measures, such as cutting its links with the British pound."

At that time, Singapore was part of the sterling bloc and the Singapore Government was warned that it could not follow Hong Kong's example and set up a foreign currency pool or Asian dollar market. Hong Kong's privilege was due to historical, legacy reasons. Singapore was warned that if it wanted to pursue this path, it might have to leave the sterling area.

Lee Kuan Yew has shared in the past, "At that time, we were newly independent. We didn't have the confidence on our own to back the Singapore dollar. So I discussed this with Hon Sui Sen and said, 'Let's go.' So we told the British, 'Okay, call off the sterling block, we are on our own.'"

While the British threat did not come to pass in the end, Singapore's financial sector was borne out of the gumption of its founding fathers. Singapore had none of the advantages which Hong Kong had at that time — namely strong links to the City of London nor the explicit backing of the Bank of England. Nevertheless, Singapore had the courage to challenge the status quo and break new ground, even when it risked upsetting the Establishment.

This same gumption and trailblazing spirit pervaded other aspects of policymaking. As an example, in the 1960s to 1970s, Singapore strived to attract multinational corporations (MNCs) to set up operations here as part of its industrialisation effort. This initiative ran counter to the conventional economic wisdom of the day. MNCs, which were widely feared at that time, exploited economies rather than enriched them. Not one to go with the flow, Singapore pursued MNCs relentlessly, and they provided the jobs and the knowledge transfer that helped upgrade the workforce.

As the domestic economy grew, the financial sector benefitted. The financial sector, in turn, had a knock-on effect on the broader economy, spurring the growth of supporting sectors like the legal and accounting professions — this helped create a virtuous circle of growth.

Singapore's financial sector flourished because the country was able to capitalise on a timezone advantage. More than that, it had qualities which have set the country apart all these years: political stability, a strong legal system, good corporate governance, physical infrastructure and an English-speaking workforce. In addition, Singapore has cultivated a reputation for being a well-regulated financial centre, and the ability of our banks to come out of successive financial crises relatively unscathed has further burnished our name.

Over the years, Singapore has also sought to deepen its financial markets — the Singapore Exchange (SGX) continues to face intense competition from Hong Kong, which has the benefit of a large China hinterland. Nevertheless, a supportive regulatory regime has enabled Singapore to become the largest real estate investment trust (REIT) market in Asia and ex-Japan, while the SGX continues to draw listings from new markets. Our derivatives exchange is one of Asia's largest with the bond market being one of the most developed in Asia. The asset management industry has grown in size and diversity, from SG$276 billion in 2000 to SG$1.82 trillion as at end 2013.

All these have been highly laudable given the prevailing challenges: talent shortage (stemming from the ease of mobility of financial sector professionals), intense competition from rival hubs such as Hong Kong, and the emergence of new ones including Shanghai, as well as a small domestic market.

Nevertheless, I am optimistic about the prospects for Singapore's financial sector. My view is that the financial services sector will become even more important for Singapore's economy moving forward, and will be crucial to drive its next phase of growth. Assuming that the economy grows at its current medium-term potential growth pace of 4 percent in the coming years, the financial sector will account for about 15 percent of the economy 10 years from now. In terms of workforce, it should employ about 7 percent of the entire workforce.

## Looking Forward

What accounts for this optimism? I believe there are megatrends that will define Asia in the years to come and Singapore is well-positioned to capture the opportunities before us. These opportunities include: A growing middle class and rising consumerism — gone are the days where goods produced in Asia are naturally shipped to the West. Asia, today, is generating more of its own demand, and this will only increase. Increasingly, Asian companies are also supplying Asian consumption demand. Consequently, there has been a shift from the traditional hub-and-spoke trade architecture of small and medium-sized enterprises (SMEs) in Asia supplying to the United States (US) or Europe, to a spaghetti mix of trade patterns arising from more end-user demand in Asia.

With the increase in connectivity in Asia, trade between China and India has grown exponentially, and China is now India's number one trading partner. Many of the largest trade corridors also either end in China or Singapore — this presents huge opportunities for banks to work with these companies across borders by helping them set up in new markets, finance supply and distribution chains, and manage currencies, risks and working capital.

Increasing consumerism will create large opportunities for consumer finance. Growth in this area is reliant on appropriate policy frameworks for consumer protection and robust infrastructure for credit underwriting and credit bureaus in particular. As an industry, we have made good progress in this area.

Second is rising affluence — Asia today is creating wealth faster than anywhere else in the world. This, coupled with the increasing funds flow from Europe and the Middle East, provide an obvious opportunity. Singapore has done well to position itself as a wealth management hub, based on a track record for safety, soundness and clockwork efficiency. Going forward, we need to continue to grow the community of asset managers, private banks and wealth advisors here.

Thirdly, as companies both big and small, begin to extend outside of their home markets, there are greater cross border flows. The age of the Asian MNC is here, and the proportion of Asian SMEs which become MNCs will only grow. Increased regionalisation is beneficial to Singapore as the nation is a hub for many Asian corporates in this part of the world.

For example, there are about 6,000 Indian companies incorporated in Singapore — the largest base of foreign companies in Singapore is from India. They are establishing trading hubs here and using Singapore as a regional centre for foreign direct investment (FDI). Most recently, Indian firms have begun thinking of Singapore as a holding company base for all their businesses. The Singapore banks are not just being looked upon as a source of financing; they also provide Indian companies a springboard to Southeast Asia, and are a conduit into China. At DBS, for example, we are able to intermediate the trade and capital flows coming from India to the East.

Singapore is also growing in stature as a major hub for a wide range of soft and hard commodities. We should continue to strengthen the banking industry's competencies so as to offer specialised financial services.

Fourth is to do with infrastructure build-up — between 2010 and 2020, the average overall infrastructure investment in Asia is expected to top US$750 billion a year. There is a huge thirst for infrastructure investment. Singapore has set up Clifford Capital, a specialist institution to plug gaps in project financing. On DBS' part, we are also working with the World Bank to identify and develop bankable projects in Asia. In addition, the World Bank's investment arm, the International Finance Corporation (IFC), has set up in Singapore its first asset management company office outside of Washington DC to co-invest in regional infrastructure projects.

Fifth is the internationalisation of the renminbi (RMB), another trend that bodes well for Singapore's financial services sector. According to Society for Worldwide Interbank Financial Telecommunication (Swift), China's yuan has become the world's seventh most-used currency for payments, overtaking both the Singapore and Hong Kong dollars. Yuan trade settlement has also expanded quickly since it first began in 2009 with the percentage of China's trade settled in yuan risen to an estimated 20 percent in November 2013, from 12 percent in 2012. Singapore has been nimble and quick to become an offshore RMB centre and this bodes well for us as China continues to internationalise its currency.

All things considered, the opportunities before us are tremendous.

Of course, as we move forward, there will be hard issues to grapple with and challenges that will require the same mettle, inventiveness and meticulous planning that have gotten us to where we are today.

To stay ahead, it is imperative that Singapore continues to build talent and management platforms that can help the financial sector manage risks and grow. The financial services sector is ultimately a people-driven business, and we already have a deep talent pool. However, while a lot has already been done to groom people in the industry, we need to continually raise the bar in training and development, such as through the Finance Industry Competency Standards programmes. The Monetary Authority of Singapore is stepping up efforts to build a strong core of Singaporean specialists and leaders in finance. At the same time, to stay relevant in the more complex financial landscape of tomorrow, Singapore must remain open to diverse talents and expertise.

We must also ask ourselves: do we really seek to embrace being a global city? For London and New York, the answer has been unequivocal. In Singapore's case, the jury is out because being a global city comes with pluses and minuses such as growing income disparity. If we choose not to be a global city, that brings into question the economic and growth model that we seek.

All in, I am bullish about Singapore's prospects as the leading financial centre in Asia and optimistic that it can even eventually be a "London", that is, become an offshore Eurozone of Asia. Apart from the megatrends that will provide tailwinds for our growth, Singapore has a strong rule of law, and most alternate sites in Asia still have some way to go in this aspect. The country is also a massive aggregator of funds, and such money flows are hard to shift.

In December 2012, about two months after inaugurating our new headquarters, DBS announced that we would be acquiring a 30 percent stake in MBFC Tower 3 for over SG$1 billion. From being the anchor tenant of MBFC Tower 3, the bank now owns a stake in the building instead. This represents our vote of confidence in Singapore and the future of our financial sector.

# Chapter 4

# SGP 4.0 — Singapore in the Artificial Intelligence Era*

*Laurence Liew*

*This article was originally published in Commentary, Volume 27 titled "SGP4.0: An Agenda" © 2018 The National University of Singapore Society. Laurence Liew is the Director for Artificial Intelligence (AI) Industry Innovation at AI Singapore.

Singapore 4.0 — the AI (Artificial Intelligence) Lap — will bring about exciting new opportunities but also challenges. Opportunities, which if seized at the right time will lead to great rewards and prosperity for Singapore. Challenges, which if not addressed may break our society and country. The new fourth generation or 4G leaders need to not only be politically savvy, but they also need to be business and technology-savvy. More importantly, they need to take intelligent and calculated risks to grasp the opportunities and challenges of "The Second Machine Age", which is a term coined by experts on the AI era, Erik Brynjolfsson and Andrew McAfee.

## State and Society's Response to Technological Change

The steam engine brought about the Industrial Revolution, and the Big Data age of the Information Revolution over the past two decades introduced us to companies such as Google, Facebook and Alibaba. But it will be AI that revolutionises the compact between government and its people; between industries and its workers.

Singapore has seen this kind of transition as factories, which used to hire thousands of workers have shifted their operations to lower-cost countries in the last decade. Globalisation and automation streamlined operations and made them easily portable across countries, often independent of the education level of the workers.

However, in the past, this displacement happened mainly to factory or other blue-collar workers. Not so in the Age of AI where the disruption will affect what we still think of as sophisticated and white-collar jobs. For example, AI systems can read X-rays and MRIs (magnetic resonance images) faster and as accurately as human radiologists; search, compile and produce legal case summaries in seconds compared to lawyers who may take days; sieve through thousands of documents and transactions to detect fraudulent transactions in audits; compute a client's risk profile to price an insurance premium in near real-time; advise a bank client on what shares or stocks to trade and/or invest in; and handle voice support calls that respond to customers' simple, routine, FAQ-type questions.

On the other hand, for each of these challenges, there are new opportunities. For example, radiologists can now focus on complex cases and reduce error rates; lawyers can now focus on analysing cases and being creative in planning how to win them; auditors can focus on complex human-to-human investigations supported by insights from the AI system; insurance companies can lower their risks, create more interesting products and offer more cost-effective policies based on individual risk profile instead of a generic profile; bank advisors can provide a more personal approach and focus on difficult or premium customers; and call operators will be relieved of responding to routine questions and can focus on difficult questions or those that require human empathy.

Most of the jobs mentioned above entail completing multiple tasks unlike those of production-line workers. In other words, AI will remove the routine, mundane and predictable tasks and allow us to focus on higher-order and higher-value tasks. A good example would be your humble SPAM engine, which is AI-driven and has helped save millions of hours from VIAGRA4U and DEAREST ONE.

We cannot stop the advance of AI, nor should we avoid it. We need to learn how to harness and even excel at AI to maximise the advantage Singapore can have in embracing it. At the same time, we have to try to minimise the negative impact of the displacement of jobs and workers. Some studies have shown that more jobs will be created by AI than jobs lost to it. Some of those jobs will require the worker to have AI skills and hence a higher level of education, but most will not.

The blue, white and grey-collar workers who do jobs that are in-between the first two categories, will need to learn how to race with machines and not against them. They will need to learn how to leverage AI tools to increase their own productivity and value; to position themselves as AI-enabled and AI-ready workers, engineers, executives and managers.

Some examples of companies that use data and AI to power their businesses include Netflix and Youtube. Closer to home, AI Singapore has within the last one year engaged with companies that are keen to undertake an AI project, including building up their own AI talent. Some of these companies are Surbana Jurong, Defence Science and Technology Agency (DSTA), Singtel, Daimler South East Asia and Johnson & Johnson. We expect to support them with up to 200 AI engineers via our AI Apprenticeship Programme initially. If Singaporeans are open enough to embrace technology and ride the wave, there will always be new job and career opportunities.

In that vein, the start-up ecosystem we have in Singapore must be one of those engines for the creation of new industries, businesses and jobs. So, it is imperative that the 4G leadership finds ways to strengthen the start-up ecosystem and encourage the creation of startup companies whether in deep tech or otherwise.

What are some other issues that will emerge with the development of AI as we try to ensure positive outcomes for jobs, wages and people?

## Universal Basic Income

There have been calls by various groups globally for governments to implement policies like Universal Basic Income (UBI), which guarantees any adult an income regardless of whether they are employed. Another group of policies are on managing robot or AI taxes.

While it is unlikely that Singapore will adopt UBI anytime soon given the strong anti-welfarist orientation of the Government, we already have policies and government programmes which, if you peel away the acronyms like CITREP, TESA and SkillsFuture, represent a limited form of UBI.

For example, today, in AI Singapore which I am part of, we have the AI Apprenticeship Programme mentioned earlier which is a nine-month programme of self-directed learning and hands-on training in skills to build and operate AI systems. The programme is funded by The Info-communications Media Development Authority's (IMDA) TESA programme and AI Singapore. The apprentices have their tuition and course fees waived, and are paid a stipend of between S$2,500 and S$3,500 per month. The stipend allows them to focus on learning a new skill and not worry about meeting daily expenses.

This approach of funding training costs, which ranges from a 70 to 100 percent subsidy and the provision of a stipend for some specific programmes is Singapore's version of UBI. The Singapore approach is measured; we do not freely provide this "UBI" — you get "UBI" only if you agree to upgrade or re-skill yourself.

This has proven to be a powerful policy and it has allowed our precious tax dollars to be spent on nudging as many as possible towards acquiring new skills and knowledge.

## Software Intellectual Property

In taxpayer-funded research, we need to review research and development (R&D) policies specifically where the intellectual property (IP) generated is software, and question policies where universities and research institutes hold on to taxpayer-funded research while making Singapore companies pay royalties for the licence to use them. It feels like these companies are being taxed twice.

Our IP policies, at least with respect to software R&D, are still based on the legacy model of closed source development where the source code is not released to anyone except under a fee-paying agreement, that is, through royalties or other commercial agreements.

However, the open source model of development and innovation has changed the economics of IP exploitation. In the open source model, the source code is shared freely with anyone under a friendly licence such as BSD, MIT or Apache 2.0. In particular, the Apache 2.0 licence is commercially friendly and has gained wide adoption.

The Apache 2.0 licence allows anyone to freely use, modify, distribute and sell a software licensed under the Apache Licence without worrying about the use of software, including patents. This is because the licence explicitly grants developers the copyright and patent of the derivative software. The rights given are perpetual, worldwide, irrevocable, but also non-exclusive.

Just look at examples such as Apache Spark, developed by UC Berkeley under a friendly open source licence, and subsequently commercialised by some of the students and original developers. Spark is now the de facto standard for big data processing and storage, and has created hundreds of thousands of jobs worldwide.

Another example is Google's Tensorflow, the most popular AI framework today which can be used for free. It has created numerous start-ups and the economic benefits that accrue are enjoyed not just by Google, but also by the whole ecosystem.

The advantage of the open source model is clear in the two examples above — people everywhere like free and good software. If the software is good, it will be adopted as the standard. Companies can then commercialise the adoption, and often the companies that succeed in commercialisation do include the original developers. After all, it is very difficult for an external party to come in and "own" the software if they are not part of the original development team or community. This community safeguard is stronger than any licence.

Back to Singapore — how much of our taxpayer-funded research has been exploited and commercialised to the likes of Spark and Tensorflow? Are our researchers in the best position to exploit the IP that has been created? Would it not be better if taxpayer-funded IP were in the hands of entrepreneurs via friendly open source licences? It will allow them to commercialise the IP in a faster and bolder fashion. It is not that our technology is not world-class. On the contrary, many are at the top across several fields. However, it is our legacy IP policies that have prevented researchers from being able to see the adoption of their IP by a critical mass of users. Instead, these languish in folders in the legal departments of some offices.

## Be Agile, Be Bold

Singapore admittedly has lost its technological edge in a few areas like e-payments and digital courts. In contrast, China's Supreme Courts already recognise blockchain-based evidence as being legally-binding. It is only recently that the Government here has embraced Agile IT development practices and open source technology.

This, after the industry has been pushing for the adoption of Agile and open source technology since 2000. While it is understandable to want stable and proven systems, there are many areas, especially in information technology, where some risks need to be taken and where we innovate fast and fail faster.

We need the 4G leadership to allow agencies like GovTech and its partners to experiment, to fail and to learn from failure and iterate again; to allow universities to experiment with innovative ways of training the next generation of engineers, developers, management, thinkers and makers.

We need the 4G leadership to allow government agencies to be bold and experiment; to take risks with Singapore start-ups. The IMDA Accreditation scheme, which validates and accredits our local start-ups and SMEs, provides a green lane for them to access to government projects. This is the right move, but we can be bolder and allow agencies wider leeway to work with our Singapore local start-up companies.

What will the situation look like when that transformation is complete? Would we be able to view "SGP 4.0" as an upgrade, an improvement, or a paradigm shift altogether? Will it be achieving something that is long overdue?

A transformation is complete when the butterfly transforms from egg to larva to pupa and finally to adult butterfly. However, for a country like Singapore, there can never be a complete transformation. Just like we encourage Singaporeans to adopt a mindset of lifelong learning, the 4G leadership must adopt a mindset of lifelong evolution and transformation for Singapore. Our transformation will never be complete since technology never stops evolving. It will mean that we must continue to evolve, transform and adapt too.

# Chapter 5

# Singapore and ASEAN: Working in Tandem to Leverage Industrial Revolution 4.0*

*Sanchita Basu Das*

*This article was originally published in Commentary, Volume 27 titled "SGP4.0: An Agenda" © 2018 The National University of Singapore Society. At the time of writing, Dr Sanchita Basu Das was Lead Researcher for Economic Affairs at the ASEAN Studies Centre of ISEAS-Yusof Ishak Institute, Singapore. She was also a Fellow with the Regional Economic Studies Programme based in the same institute.

In the era of Industrial Revolution 4.0 (IR 4.0), technological advancement is fast changing the way people live and businesses operate. Digital applications, like Uber and Airbnb, are enabling people to travel and book hotels through the Internet. E-platforms, such as Amazon and Lazada, are helping people to shop through web-based technology. E-payment schemes, similar to PayNow, Nets, are allowing people to transfer money through Internet networks, thus encouraging them to go cashless. Netflix is bringing online entertainment to people's computers and hand-held devices.

The adoption of digital and smart technology has become an imperative for companies to raise productivity. 3-D printing is enabling automotive firms to produce and deliver parts to car manufacturers. Development of the Internet of Things (IoT) is helping companies to connect the entire value chain of production and distribution across multiple stages and geography. Blockchain technology is providing a digital platform that allows transactions to be made across a secure network. Apart from these, there are several other technologies, such as artificial intelligence, robotics, autonomous vehicles, cloud computing, that have broader application across countries and industries.

Thus, the digital transformation of IR 4.0 is broadly regarded as a technology-driven revolution that has disrupted the traditional way of conducting business and consuming products. It has also disrupted the way a country is governed. While on one hand, new technologies are bringing the producers and consumers closer in an efficient and timely manner, thereby raising productivity; on the other hand, it is raising challenges in terms of privacy issues, social inequality and labour displacement due to automation. In this context, it becomes important for countries to create an enabling environment surrounding IR 4.0 to harness new opportunities for people and businesses, while safeguarding them from the negative fallout of it.

Singapore, thus, embarked on its journey called the Smart Nation Initiative in 2014 to transform the city-state through adoption of efficient technology and digital innovation. It did not stop with its vision of use of technology only within its national boundary.

During the ASEAN Chairmanship of 2018, Singapore worked with other member countries to ensure that there will be cooperation in technology-driven areas, such as e-commerce, customs, innovation and the development of smart cities across Southeast Asia.

## Singapore and Its Smart Nation Initiative

Singapore has identified the "digital economy" as a future pathway to its economic success. It adopted the Smart Nation Initiative not only to enhance use of digital or Information Communication Technology (ICT) in people's daily activities but also to explore new growth opportunities in the emergent digital space. The initiative took an integrated approach and focused on five key areas, which were transport, home and environment, business productivity, health and enabled ageing, and public sector service, and provided enabling factors in the form of facilitating research collaboration, encouraging innovation and upgrading or introducing new education programmes.

The key aspect of Singapore's Smart Nation Initiative is its focus on economic development. As noted in a speech by Prime Minister Lee Hsien Loong in 2014, the Smart Nation Initiative is likely to generate data, information and information technologies (IT) that can be used to raise economic productivity and develop new business opportunities.[1] The initiative deployed public resources in building smart nation capabilities. It made investments in research and development through agencies like the National Research Foundation, through collaboration between government agencies and universities, and the private sector. It introduced new ICT training and education courses for the people so as to develop more IT professionals and data analysts.

Despite a well thought-out comprehensive initiative, the pace of adoption of new technology across different industries and firms in

---

[1] Lee, Hsien Loong, "Transcript of Prime Minister Lee Hsien Loong's Speech at Smart Nation Launch on 24 November," Prime Minister's Office, https://www.pmo.gov.sg/newsroom/transcript-prime-minister-lee-hsien-loongs-speech-smart-nation-launch-24-november

the city-state remains uneven.[2] Often, it is found that companies lack understanding of the concept of IR 4.0 and hence lack the capacity to draw up business strategies and roadmaps. They are uncertain of the benefits of adopting IR 4.0 in their activities. There are also feelings of uncertainty among manufacturers about the ways to implement IR 4.0 in their production operations. For companies that have embarked on their journey of IR 4.0, the knowledge about IR 4.0 remains limited to the top management and is often not diffused across wider workforce.

In this situation, the Economic Development Board (EDB) of Singapore developed the Singapore Smart Industry Readiness Index to "strike a balance between technical rigour and practical applicability".[3] It outlined three core building blocks — technology, process and organisation — that are said to be essential to adopting IR 4.0 in business operations successfully. The index is believed to help companies to understand IR 4.0 and find ways to benefit from it.

Singapore strongly believes that IR 4.0 offers immense opportunities for its people and businesses. According to a Boston Consulting Group study, IR 4.0 can enhance total manufacturing output by S$36 billion, improve labour productivity by 30 percent and generate 22,000 additional jobs in Singapore by 2024.[4] Embracing technological transformation can help the city-state cement its position as a global hub for several manufacturing and services industries.

## Forging Regional Cooperation in Digital Economy

During its 2018 ASEAN chairmanship, Singapore seized the opportunity to promote digital innovation as a way not only to uphold its

---

[2] "The Singapore Smart Industry Readiness Index: Catalysing the Transformation of Manufacturing," EDB Singapore, https://www.gov.sg/~/sgpcmedia/media_releases/edb/press_release/P-20171113-1/attachment/The%20Singapore%20Smart%20Industry%20Readiness%20Index%20-%20Whitepaper_final.pdf, 3.

[3] Ibid, 4.

[4] Ibid, 7.

own economic development, but also as a means to boost resilience in the region. For the city-state, the ASEAN economies, with their combined population size of 630 million, a rising middle class and a high percentage of Internet users, are ready for IT-enabled products and services.

Lately, as a region, ASEAN has been grabbing attention for e-commerce or Internet-based economic activities. According to AT Kearney, the e-retail market size of ASEAN-6 countries is US$7 billion, with Singapore accounting for the maximum at 25 percent, followed by Malaysia and Indonesia.[5] Although this is low when compared to other markets of the United States (US), Japan and China, the leading indicators prevalent currently in the member economies point to its immense potential in the future.[6] Indeed, more than 50 percent of ASEAN's total population is below 30 years of age (compared to 39 percent of the population in East Asia and 34 percent of the population in Europe). Of the total population size of 630 million, the region has 480 million Internet users and 700 million mobile phone users. In addition, the countries have established an economic community for better integration on trade and investment in 2015, which raises the prospects further. The ASEAN countries have long been paying attention to cross-border trade activities. While the countries have reduced their border tariffs significantly, it is the trade facilitation that continues to be work-in-progress. The countries have made commitments to establish their e-customs facility, also known as National Single Window (NSW) that will be connected at the regional level (ASEAN Single Window or ASW), to enable paperless exchange of trade-related information. This is expected to generate efficiency and predictability for traders and businesses in the region. According to a survey project by USAID, companies are estimated to be able to save US$60 per consignment or around 8 percent of the current system when

[5] "Lifting the Barriers to E-Commerce in ASEAN," A.T. Kearney, https://www.atkearney.co.uk/documents/10192/5540871/Lifting+the+Barriers+to+E-Commerce+in+ASEAN.pdf, p. 2.
[6] Ibid, 4.

they use the ASW for exchange of government and commercial documents.[7]

Despite such benefits and prospects from increased digital connectivity, there is apprehension about regional cooperation, especially when it concerns job creation, cyber-security and the digital divide both within and across the ASEAN nations.

The World Bank in its 2016 World Development Report (WDR) provided an answer to this. It mentioned that although there is a rapid proliferation of digital technologies across the world, the digital dividends, described as broader development benefits from using them, have lagged behind.[8] Also the aggregate benefits are unevenly distributed.

The report subsequently argued that it is crucial to narrow the digital divide. This not only implies greater Internet access but also widespread digital adoption. It is vital for countries to work on their "analogue complements", which involves strengthening regulations and standards for businesses to operate in, upgrading skills to match the demand of the new economy and developing supportive institutions.

## Digital Divide in ASEAN

If we examine the performance of the ASEAN countries on some of the parameters of digital connectivity, it becomes clear why ASEAN has yet to leverage the digital revolution fully.

At the end of 2015, Internet users per 100 of the population varied widely across ASEAN countries. Singapore had the highest at 82.1, followed by Brunei and Malaysia at 71. Cambodia and Laos were at the tail end of 19 and 18 respectively. Even the percentage of firms using electronic mail (email) to interact with clients or

---

[7] "USAID ASEAN Single Window Project. ASEAN Single Window - Potential Impact Survey 2012," ASEAN Single Window, http://asw.asean.org/multimedia/outreach-material/item/asw-impact-survet-booklet, 9.

[8] "Digital Dividends World Development Report 2016," World Bank Group, http://documents.worldbank.org/curated/en/896971468194972881/pdf/102725-PUB-Replacement-PUBLIC.pdf, 2.

suppliers varied. Less than 25 percent of Lao firms used email in their business operation, compared to 80 percent for the Philippines and 91 percent for Vietnam. The mobile Internet download speed in Singapore was 16.8 Mbit/s, vis-à-vis 2.5 for Malaysia, 1.04 for Indonesia, 0.9 for Thailand, and 0.4 for Myanmar.

ASEAN governments are increasingly using digital technologies for public service delivery. These include digital identification of people, tax filing, government procurement, customs and others. However, there are wide variations in the applications and the benefits are not well-diffused. Singapore, as the most digitally advanced country in the region, leverages data analytics and digital platforms for faster and well-integrated policy decisions. Indonesia has adopted e-procurement for government contracts, but is yet to meet its objectives of improved facility and infrastructure. Finally, development of one-stop e-customs facility remains a work-in-progress for many of the ASEAN countries.

Also, the role of human skills is of utmost importance in a digital economy. Unfortunately, the biggest challenge facing ASEAN countries lies in the gap in digital capability. According to the WDR, this gap originates from two factors — those of business climate and the quality of human resource. Although the ASEAN countries have improved over time in their overall ease of doing business, there is still a wide variation. Singapore tops the chart among ASEAN countries and even the world, followed by Malaysia and Thailand. Laos, Cambodia and Myanmar fall towards the bottom end of 190 countries ranked by the World Bank.

It is important for the less developed ASEAN countries to enforce laws and regulations to ensure easy entry and exit of firms and to create an open business regime to encourage competition. The lack of infrastructure, especially highways, rail network, warehouse and storage, hampers growth of e-commerce. Even for the advanced ASEAN countries, stringent regulations in the wake of disruptive technologies make it difficult for digital enterprises to enter new markets and achieve economies of scale. Regarding human resources, Singapore leads the pack of ASEAN countries in the Human Development Index Ranking. But countries like

Myanmar, Cambodia and Laos are challenged by their resource quality. In the Human Development Indices and Indicators 2018 statistics, the available data for most recent year in the span of years from 2006-2017 states that for Singapore, 79.4 percent of its population aged 25 and above had at least secondary education, while the proportion for Indonesia is 48.8, Laos is 39.2 and Myanmar is 25.8.[9]

Thus, the challenges that ASEAN countries face in seeking to fully benefit from the digital economy remain formidable.

In the past few years, ASEAN has announced several initiatives, ranging from building infrastructure to trading in information technology products. In 2018 particularly, ASEAN drafted a framework document on e-commerce that covers issues like customs regulations, logistics, online security, data flows and payment solutions. ASEAN launched the ASW with five countries — Indonesia, Malaysia, Singapore, Thailand and Vietnam — and the rest are working their way to joining the live operation in the near future. The 10 countries have also endorsed the ASEAN Smart Cities Network (ASCN) initiative, which will be a collaborative platform for a selected 26 cities to exchange best practices and urban solutions. The overarching objective around all these initiatives is to leverage IR 4.0 to improve lives and employment prospects of the people. It is to help businesses, particularly the small- and medium-sized enterprises (SMEs) tap the opportunities presented through regional cooperation and digital advancement in ASEAN.

## Conclusion

Digital technologies are rapidly spreading across countries and industries around the world. These have immense potential to raise income levels and offer better quality of life for people. These also have capacity to help businesses lower transaction costs and thereby boost efficiency and productivity over time.

[9] "Human Development Indices and Indicators 2018 Statistical Update," United Nations Development Programme, http://hdr.undp.org/sites/default/files/2018_human_development_statistical_update.pdf, 54–56.

However, wider use of technology comes with its own pitfalls. It can raise challenges in terms of privacy issues, socio-economic inequality and labour displacement in the long run. To balance the gains and losses, governments need to take an integrated and comprehensive approach to their policymaking. They need to look beyond the national boundaries and work with other countries to multiply the benefits and curb the drawback from the use of technology and automation.

To this end, Singapore has embarked on its Smart Nation Initiative to harness opportunities that might result from the city-state's progressively technology-driven and knowledge-based economy. It has identified focus areas and provided enablers in terms of investments in research and development, and education to attain a set of policy objectives.

Going forward, the fourth generation leaders in Singapore should pay more attention to people. While they should safeguard the citizens' interests from the effects of job disruption and lower wages, they should also stay focused on training people with the necessary skills to benefit from the digital revolution. The leaders should re-double their efforts at working with the country's SMEs to impart knowledge and strengthen appropriate digital adoption programmes to enable them to ride and gain from the IR 4.0 wave.

Simultaneously, Singapore needs to work with other ASEAN members to increase digital connectivity in the region. In 2018, the 10 countries agreed to provide an enabling environment for e-commerce operation in the region and have decided to collaborate on innovation among start-ups and SMEs. The initiative to create an ASEAN network of smart cities is also a way to leverage data and technology to offer efficiency and improve the quality of life going forward.

Indeed, as IR 4.0 is creating major disruption in the way people live or operate business, Singapore and ASEAN are strategically working and navigating challenges to reap benefits from it while we safeguard interests for an innovative and resilient society in the future.

# Chapter 6

# Singapore's Interest in LNG and Becoming a Regional Gas Hub*

*Lee Tzu Yang*

*This article was originally published in Commentary: Volume 23 titled "The Uneasy and Unchartered Road Ahead" © 2014 The National University of Singapore Society. At the time of writing, Lee Tzu Yang was the Chairman of Shell Companies in Singapore and had worked with the energy and chemicals group since 1979 in a range of different markets.

Asia has entered a historic phase of development that will have an impact on the way it uses energy. Citizens in emerging economies are buying their first refrigerators, cars, washing machines and all other consumer goods that are taken for granted in developed economies. The same countries are undergoing rapid industrialisation and urbanisation. These trends suggest a lot more energy will be used, which means more supply will have to be produced fairly quickly.

At Shell, teams of economists, engineers and scientists have been developing, over the last 40 years, a range of plausible futures and their challenging implications for our energy system, including for Asia. We share this thinking with governments, researchers, academe and the public. Our latest edition, called New Lens Scenarios, projects that energy demand could rise by as much as 80 percent by 2050. The scenarios also highlight the shift in economic influence from the West to the East. China and India together will account for the majority of energy demand growth in the next two decades.

Asia is increasingly dependent on energy imports at a time of high and volatile oil prices. According to the Asian Development Bank (ADB), most Asian countries will produce less than half the energy they need by 2035, and many will produce only a tiny fraction. The region will have to rely heavily on energy imports for decades to come.

This tremendous need for energy will put more stress on our water and food systems, as well as on the climate and environment. All these resources are tightly woven — nearly all forms of energy production require water — energy is needed to move and treat water; while producing food requires both energy and water.

Increased energy needs have also led to rising concerns about greenhouse gas emissions. On existing emissions trends, the world will far exceed the average temperature rise of 2 degrees Celsius regarded as the limit to avoid the worse effects of climate change. Asia's governments are also increasingly facing mounting public pressure to tackle chronic urban pollution and to clean up the air.

Due to the sheer scale of our energy needs, the scenarios project that fossil fuels are expected to continue to supply the majority of energy for decades to come. They expect fossil fuel consumption to rise in energy terms by about one-third over the next two decades. By 2060, fossil fuels are still likely to meet around 60 percent of global energy demand, down from about 80 percent today.

The team also estimates that by 2035, the world's renewable energy sources could grow by at least 60 percent or even double. By 2060, renewable energy could supply up to four times more energy than today, which would be a staggering rate of expansion.

Significantly, natural gas will become the most important energy source globally by the 2030s. The International Energy Agency (IEA) estimates there is enough technically available gas to last more than 230 years at today's consumption levels. Gas can be cooled to a liquid state, i.e. liquefied natural gas (LNG) and shipped across oceans. LNG is increasingly being used to help countries meet demand while increasing energy security, because its supply is becoming more abundant and diverse. In the first decade of this century, LNG demand has doubled and it is expected to double again within this decade.

In Asia, gas demand has been rising dramatically, particularly as Asia's urban populations continue to expand. In 2012, Asia represented 46 percent of global inter-regional gas trade, up from 40 percent the year before, according to the IEA. Asia overtook Organisation for Economic Co-operation and Development (OECD) Europe, the then largest importing region accounting for 45 percent of global gas imports. Asia now imports almost four times more LNG than Europe.

Most of the natural gas growth in Asia Pacific will be consumed in the power and industrial sectors, according to the IEA, with the power sector set to be dominant for the next four years. The two most mature natural gas markets in Asia Pacific are Japan and Taiwan. Both markets are nearly exclusively supplied by LNG. In 2011, they consumed 87 percent of the LNG delivered to Asia although the IEA says demand growth is likely to shift to China and India.

The region's LNG trade is set to grow as infrastructure is built in more countries. Pakistan, the Philippines, Sri Lanka and Vietnam have announced plans to build regasification terminals for LNG imports. Indonesia, Thailand, Malaysia and Singapore are already importing LNG. Given that there has been limited progress on intra-regional pipeline infrastructure promoting pipeline-supplied natural gas trade, there is still more room for the LNG trade to develop. Given the slow pace of the intra-regional effort, the region might look to more regional co-operation between governments to allow domestic gas prices to reflect international price movements, and in this way, encourage a free and liquid traded-gas market.

## Singapore's Role

Against this backdrop, Singapore is positioning itself to benefit from this historic inflexion point in energy and Asian growth. It has calculated that the region's potential demand for cleaner energy, gas in particular, will rise exponentially and has taken initial steps to build its position.

Singapore first announced plans for a world-scale LNG terminal in 2006, started building the facility in 2010 and took its first commercial delivery in 2013. This will help enhance energy security by diversifying energy supply from piped gas from Indonesia and Malaysia, which currently provide the gas for generating electricity.

Singapore's LNG import terminal has initial throughput capacity of 3.5 million tonnes per year, which is expected to expand to 9 million tonnes per year in the future. This is to ensure that supplies are secured for the country and to trade in rapidly expanding gas use within Asia. Beyond its domestic remit, the terminal will be used for storage and LNG re-exports, underscoring Singapore's ambition to become the regional energy hub as Asia's gas demand and trade grows.

Due to its strategic geographic location, Singapore has one of the best prospects in Asia of becoming a gas hub. Singapore is located between gas-exporting powerhouses in the Middle East, Australasia and gas-hungry Asia, particularly China, Japan, South

Korea and Taiwan. With frequent calls on ports in these countries, tankers can refill in gas-producing areas such as Australia, Brunei or Indonesia, enabling trade with Singapore on their way to the Middle East. This has the potential to transform patterns for the Asian gas trade.

The historic free market approach to the energy sector, combined with clear regulation and a solid legal framework in Singapore, is an important winning condition for its gas hub ambitions. In 2001, the Government decoupled commercial activities from transportation activities in the gas sector, to enable better competition for gas prices as well as to more accurately reflect market forces. It also introduced wholesale pricing for natural gas so that re-exports from Singapore may be competitively priced. Third-party access to gas infrastructure in Singapore has been guaranteed since 2008.

Singapore also has the financial infrastructure to support gas trading. By 2012, at least 14 companies with LNG trading or marketing desks, including BP, Gazprom, Shell, Vitol Group and GDF Suez were present in Singapore. Critical to shaping Singapore's hub ambitions will be continued support from the Government for the free market approach to ensure continued interest from major gas players.

Also key to these ambitions is the continued development of the Singapore gas terminal in both capacity and operational excellence, to ensure world-class efficiency and competitive costs. This will support not only trading ambitions but the reliability of competitive gas supply to the market in Singapore.

## The Region

The global trade of LNG is increasingly connecting markets, but there are still significant regional aspects to the gas and LNG industry. Gas in the United States has developed trading around hubs tied into piped gas infrastructure, and is well known for its "Henry Hub" price point in Louisiana. Europe's gas market is a hybrid of oil-linked contracts and a number of long-established as well as new gas hubs. These regions are dynamically growing short-term and spot LNG sales, over-the-counter sales and smaller volumes of shorter durations, in addition to the typical long-term contracts.

LNG in Asia has historically been sold on the basis of long-term oil-linked contracts. According to the IEA, 88 percent of natural gas traded in Asia in 2010 was priced by linkage to oil. Asian growth in LNG demand has coincided with a period of rising oil prices, resulting in LNG prices growing in tandem. This has created a debate on whether oil-linked pricing is best for the future, and questions whether Asia should also develop hub prices for gas as in Europe and the United States.

A key point in this debate is the difference in current gas prices between the United States and Asia, which appears significant. At current oil prices, Japanese long-term LNG price averages an estimated $16/MMBtu. The Japanese earthquake of 11 March, 2011, which eventually resulted in a shutdown of nearly 50GW of nuclear power, has further increased Japan's reliance on imported oil and LNG. In parallel, the United States shale gas phenomenon has driven down "Henry Hub" gas prices. While prices in these regions may seem to differ considerably, the differences are better understood after adjusting for the cost of liquefaction, transportation and regasification to trade from one region to the other. The residual difference would work out to be less dramatic.

Singapore is a highly viable location for a gas hub. While there are elements to hub pricing which are attractive to the region, other contributing factors that are needed — market liquidity and transparency; depth and breadth of trades; and a significant degree of government regulatory co-operation across Asia on energy that so far, have not been present. While Singapore can play a leading role in creating this, there are many next steps which depend on others.

## Conclusion

In order to develop a competitive and secure supply of energy, Singapore has embarked on growing the LNG sector. The development of interest from a diverse range of world class LNG players will be important, as will the demonstration of operational excellence by the Singapore terminal to be best-in-class in flexibility and costs. The debate on LNG pricing is unfolding and will play a part in how the gas trade develops in the region.

For the development of Singapore as a gas hub, in addition to the domestic factors more within the control of Singapore, the pace of progress is also dependent on world and regional changes. Most critically, these include the ability and willingness of regional players to co-operate and create the conditions for an effective integrated gas supply infrastructure with aligned regulatory frameworks. Singapore can prepare to be in a pre-eminent position to play this role when the time is right.

The extent to which Singapore develops its role as a gas hub will, in turn, support its objective of having a secure and competitive energy sector.

## Epilogue by Author

The energy scene since 2014, when this article was written, has experienced an increased drive for decarbonisation through both technological and fiscal measures, and large investments in new renewable energy, as the international community strives to agree on managing greenhouse gases. This has been complicated by geopolitical tensions and a pandemic, with attendant impacts on energy demand and how it is supplied. The projected growth from various sources at the time of this article needs to be moderated. Notwithstanding these uncertainties, it remains true that human development in emerging economies needs more energy, and much of that is in Asia.

In the fossil fuel mix, natural gas has lower carbon and will continue to play a significant role even as the world seeks to develop a range of renewables. Singapore is ramping up its sourcing of solar energy, but power generation, domestically, is largely fuelled by LNG for electricity. Having invested in the physical, maritime and financial infrastructure, Singapore continues to be well positioned to grow the trade in LNG beyond our shores.

# The Environment

# Chapter 7

# Singapore's City in Nature: More than 50 Years of Greening*

*Kenneth Er and Leong Chee Chiew*

*This article was originally published in Commentary: Volume 22 titled "The Idea of Singapore" © 2013 The National University of Singapore Society. Kenneth Er was involved in the development of Gardens by the Bay and was previously Assistant Chief Executive Officer (Corporate Development Services) in National Parks Board (NParks). Dr Leong Chee Chiew has been involved in the development and management of the Garden City since 1983. He was the Deputy Chief Executive Officer (Professional Development Services) and Commissioner of Parks & Recreation, NParks.

## From Garden City to a City in Nature

On 16 June 1963, founding Prime Minister (PM) Lee Kuan Yew planted a *Cratoxylum formosum* at the Farrer Circus. This signified the launch of Singapore's greening movement, a sustained effort that has spanned more than 50 years and transformed Singapore into a premier tropical garden city. The tree-planting site at Farrer Circus was replaced by road development, but has since been restored with the planting of seven *Cratoxylum formosum* trees in 2016 to mark the significance of the site. This reflects the rapid rate of urban renewal and the challenge of balancing development with urban greening in Singapore.

Singapore's growth as a Garden City did not come by chance. As some would argue, this was a case of environmental possibilism — with the urban environment being an engineered landscape and a product of "Man's intervention in Nature". It is the archetypal demonstration of the Singapore Government's efficiency in planning and its pragmatic approach in governance. Focused on liveability and guided by clear environmental and social objectives, the aim was to plant as much vegetation as quickly as possible, while parks and green spaces were established to further soften the landscape and provide places for recreation.

The Garden City vision laid the foundation for our subsequent transformation into a City in a Garden. This was a period of refinement involving a concerted effort to intensify greenery in the urban environment, including on buildings. The aim was to connect the greenery into a landscape matrix that enveloped and permeated the city-state, which would bring about ecological and recreational benefits. Also, more attention was paid to outreach and engagement programmes.

In 2020, the National Parks Board (NParks) unveiled plans to advance Singapore into a City in Nature, with the objective of restoring nature into the landscape to overcome the long-term challenges of urbanisation and climate change. Building on our achievements as a biophilic City in a Garden, NParks will work together with the community to ensure that Singapore remains liveable and we can continue to enjoy clean water, clean air, and the health benefits that come from living with nature.

This chapter reflects on the key success factors that brought about the Garden City and shares the optimism ahead as Singapore seeks to transform itself into a City in Nature.

## Growing the Garden City

In 1992, the United Nations lauded Singapore for its green policies and the integration of environmental concerns into development policies. In 2008, Dr Ahmed Djoghlaf, then Executive Secretary of the United Nations Convention on Biological Diversity, visited Singapore and was so pleased with Singapore's conservation model that he remarked to the local media, "I am extremely impressed by Singapore and never imagined that you would have such greenery and nature in the heart of one of the most populated cities in the world. Singapore is already going in the right direction but my plea is that the experience you have accumulated, you share with the world and your neighbours." NParks was also awarded the UNESCO Sultan Qaboos prize in 2017 for its efforts in environmental preservation. The success of the Garden City vision came about because of several factors, of which four are highlighted here.

Rooftop Garden in public housing estate (Edgefield Plains)

## Strong Government Commitment

When founding PM Lee launched Singapore's greening movement in 1963, he saw this as both an economic and social imperative. The Garden City vision was a deliberate strategy to differentiate Singapore from other developing countries by turning it into a tropical garden city with well-maintained greenery. He believed that this was the most cost-effective way to impress visiting dignitaries and investors the commitment and efficiency of the government. He also felt that this was a good way to raise the morale of the people and give them a sense of pride in their environment and in Singapore.[1]

PM Lee did not just provide the vision but was personally involved in the greening of Singapore. This was best illustrated when Singapore hosted the Commonwealth Prime Ministers' Conference in 1971. He directed the greening of the city-state by expediting the planting of roadside trees and shrubs, and providing a budget of $1.2 million for this. He also set up the Garden City Action Committee (GCAC) to plan, co-ordinate and implement greening measures to spruce up the city for the conference. The GCAC would continue thereafter to co-ordinate efforts amongst public sector agencies to transform Singapore into a Garden City. This was instrumental as the Garden City initiative would require a whole-of-government effort and silos across agencies had to be broken down for this to succeed.

The successful transformation of Singapore into a Garden City in a relatively short period of time is attributed to the personal attention from the political leaders, as well as the ability of agencies to work across boundaries. As we transition into a City in Nature, the Government continues to emphasise the importance of greenery in providing a high-quality living environment to a growing population, and in responding to increasingly complex challenges of rapid urbanisation and climate change.

---

[1] Lee, Kuan Yew, *From Third World to First: The Singapore Story: 1965–2000* (Singapore: Singapore Press Holdings and Times Editions, 2000).

## Greenery Provision as Part of National Development

Singapore is probably one of the few countries where the government agency mandated to manage and develop its green assets resides within a Ministry that is responsible for infrastructural development and not the environment. There are good reasons for this and it did, in fact, contribute immensely to the development of the Garden City.

In the late 1960s, the Parks & Trees Unit was set up within the Roads Branch of the Public Works Department (PWD) in the Ministry of National Development (MND). This later became the Parks and Recreation Department (PRD), which was merged under NParks in 1996. The presence of the Parks & Trees Unit within the PWD allowed for a sustained effort in roadside tree planting and provided much-needed close co-ordination in the development of a road code which incorporated tree planting.

The transition from PRD to NParks marked a paradigm shift in the emphasis on the role of parks, gardens and greenery in Singapore. In the years leading to the formation of NParks, the development and management of green spaces was seen largely from the viewpoint of green infrastructure. Instead, NParks focused

Streetscape — Mandai Road

on the value proposition of parks, gardens, nature reserves and green spaces from the viewpoint of conservation, research and education as well as the promotion of leisure lifestyle and the social well-being of Singaporeans and residents. This shift in focus was greatly facilitated by the close working relationship between NParks and the Urban Redevelopment Authority (URA). Since they were the same Ministry, there was a greater alignment of vision that the provision of green spaces for recreation and the safeguarding of our natural heritage were critical to making Singapore more distinctive and liveable. The Parks and Waterbodies Plan in 2001, which mapped out a vision for the next 40 to 50 years, is the result of that close working relationship. For the benefit of future generations, the Concept Plan aimed at doubling green spaces from 2,500 hectares at the time to 4,500 hectares. Subsequent master plans set aside increasingly more land for green spaces, so much so that today, NParks safeguards more than 7,800 hectares of green spaces across Singapore.

Aside from centralising greenery provision within the ambit of the MND, there was a clear direction from the onset that the provision of greenery was part of national infrastructure development. The Parks and Trees Act, which was enacted in Parliament in 1975, provided legislation that stipulated the provision of green verges along roadsides and the conservation of mature trees in the Tree Conservation Areas around Bukit Timah and Changi. The Act was later revised to allow for a broader stipulation for greenery provision, and the current legislation provides for the planting, maintenance and conservation of trees and plants within national parks, nature reserves, tree conservation areas, heritage road green buffers and other specified areas.

## Continual Professional Development and Innovation

Central to the sustained growth and maintenance of the Garden City was the strong pursuit of professional development and a culture of innovation. In the early years, research teams were sent overseas to source for fast-growing tropical trees that would green up the city. This was coupled by the greening of concrete structures such as retaining walls and flyovers with an ivy-like creeper, *Ficus pumila*. Bougainvillea was introduced so that this would cover the vehicular impact guardrails. Planting troughs were also creatively designed on overhead bridges, so that Bougainvillea and other flowering climbers could adorn and soften these structures.

The spirit of professional development continues to prevail. The Centre for Urban Greenery and Ecology (CUGE) was established in 2007 to develop expertise in the industry and share knowledge on urban greenery and ecology. This filled a much-needed gap in the training of horticulturists and arborists within NParks and the industry. Standards were also set and benchmarked internationally. For example, the Certified Arborist Programme, a certification accredited with the International Society of Arboriculture, was introduced to ensure that the highest standards in tree care are maintained. As we transition into a City in Nature, NParks continues to raise standards in the industry by incorporating technology into tree maintenance. NParks is digitalising its management of arboriculture, horticulture, parks and facilities for greater productivity and efficiency and to transform the landscape industry as a whole.

Recognising the need to overcome severe land constraints in order to provide a high quality of life for our residents, NParks looked to innovation. The Park Connector Network (PCN) was first conceived in the early 1990s to link nature reserves, gardens, parks and other green spaces into a vast recreational network. Land in drainage reserves that was otherwise idle was used to create island-wide paths for cycling and hiking and the planting of trees and shrubs. This was subsequently extended into road reserves. By planting species that were attractive to birds, butterflies and dragonflies, the PCN also provided ecological connectivity between fragmented areas of high biodiversity. More than 340 kilometres of park connectors have been completed today, and this will be expanded to 500 kilometres by 2030 to give Singaporeans recreational options beyond what one would expect of a small island-state.

Over the years, a concerted effort has been made to not only restore our natural habitats within the nature reserves, but to ensure that the biodiversity within the reserves would persist over time. For this to succeed, animals and plants need to be able to disperse between insular habitat remnants. This ensures the exchange of genetic material between populations and insures against extinctions due to the outbreak of diseases or natural forces such as wind and fire. As part of a holistic conservation approach, NParks has established a network of nature parks that surround Singapore's nature reserves. These nature parks provide expanded habitats for native flora and fauna and help to buffer the reserves from the impact of nearby development. The nature way network is another effort to increase ecological connectivity between green spaces. Designed to replicate the natural, multitiered structure of local forests, nature ways along roads function as ecological corridors. NParks aims to increase the nature way and nature park networks to 300 km and 550 ha, respectively, by 2030.

Jurong Lake Gardens

Progress of efforts to enhance urban biodiversity, such as by creating island-wide ecological corridors and habitats, is monitored using the Singapore Index on Cities' Biodiversity. Developed in collaboration with the Secretariat of the Convention on Biological Diversity, the Singapore Index is used by cities worldwide as a self-assessment tool for native biodiversity in the city, ecosystem services provided by biodiversity in the city, and governance and management of biodiversity in the city.

Yet another example of innovation is the newly opened Jurong Lake Gardens. The centrepiece of the Jurong Lake District, which is envisioned to be a smart and sustainable district of the future, the Gardens provides an apt environment for testing new technology. Some of the technologies which will be utilised at the Gardens are a waste-to-energy system to convert horticultural waste into electricity and an Integrated Management System (IMS) to monitor and control multiple systems such as irrigation, lighting and carpark management in an automated and centralised manner.

Community in Bloom

## Long-standing Partnership with Community

The PRD and NParks have had a long association with the community, which played many roles to help establish the Garden City and will be a key component of our successful transition into a City in Nature. Community stewardship is encouraged through several initiatives. A good example is the Community in Bloom programme which was established in 2005. The objective was to inculcate a gardening culture in Singapore. Since its inception, more than 1,600 community gardens have been established in private and public residential estates, schools, hospitals and even office precincts. This has proven to be successful as people from all walks of life come together to form gardening interest groups and beautify their community gardens. NParks has also engaged the community to become stewards of nature through our Community in Nature Biodiversity Watch series. Started in 2015, this popular citizen science initiative engages the public to survey biodiversity in green spaces across Singapore, and the data collected helps to inform our conservation strategies.

In addition to creating a greater sense of ownership amongst the community, NParks has been proactive in engaging non-government organisations (NGOs) on nature conservation. At a

Sungei Buloh Wetland Reserve

time when engagement with NGOs was rare, NParks worked with the Nature Society (Singapore) (NSS) to conserve 85 hectares of mangrove wetlands at Sungei Buloh as a bird sanctuary in 1988. Sungei Buloh eventually became a nature reserve in 2000. Applying scientific study to establish the complementary habitats in Sungei Buloh and Mandai Mangrove and Mudflat led to the announcement in 2018 that the Mangrove and Mudflat will be conserved as a nature park. Another example is our Friends of the Parks initiative, in which we engage localised communities and stakeholders to play an active role in promoting responsible use of the parks, and to take part in the design, development and management of Singapore's parks and green spaces.

## Towards Becoming a City in Nature

The future is one of optimism. NParks' plans to advance Singapore into a City in Nature will strengthen our resilience to the impact of climate change through nature-based solutions. The vision comprises seven key areas: safeguarding our nature reserves and extending our natural capital by expanding our nature park network; curating the landscapes in gardens and

parks to make them more natural; restoring nature into the urban landscape to mitigate the harshness of the built environment; strengthening ecological connectivity between green spaces; safeguarding public health, animal health and welfare, and conservation of biodiversity; deepening our science and technology capabilities to inform our strategic and operational decision-making; and expanding outreach programmes to communities, schools and individuals to encourage them to become stewards of greenery and biodiversity.

Building upon the foundations of the Garden City and City in a Garden, we will continue to intensify greenery as we focus further on integrating nature into the urban ecosystem. This is far more challenging than merely beautifying the city with amenity plantings for shade and to soften the harshness of the urban environment. It moves the paradigm from biodiversity conservation within the nature reserves alone to conservation through habitat restoration and enhancement within the landscape matrix that also comprises parks and gardens, park connectors, nature ways, nature parks and streetscapes. The focus on community gardening goes further to tap on the gardening movement to foster a community spirit, build social resilience and bring together residents of all ages to help make Singapore a City in Nature. The energy and enthusiasm of the community is also being harnessed as citizen scientists of all ages and walks of life become stewards of nature through the Community in Nature programme. In tandem with this effort to engage the community in co-creation, the development of a Round Island Route as an extension of the Park Connector Network seeks to connect not just parks, but communities. This will capture the imagination of Singaporeans and bring a nation of people of different generations together. Last but not least, the Singapore Botanic Gardens, a rich repository of botanical discoveries in this part of the world and a bastion of heritage and shared memories amongst Singaporeans, will continue to be promoted as a world-class botanical institution and our first UNESCO World Heritage Site.

As a City in Nature, Singapore will continue to differentiate itself as a highly liveable city which is able to mitigate global challenges of urbanisation and climate change. Singapore will illustrate how forward planning, innovation, science and community ownership and stewardship can overcome severe land constraints to sustain an environment rich in biodiversity and nature. Our island-state will remain truly unique.

# Chapter 8

# 500 Shades of Green*

*Geh Min*

* This article was originally published in Commentary: Volume 23 titled "Singapore Challenged: The Uneasy and Unchartered Road Ahead" © 2014 The National University of Singapore Society. Dr Geh Min was President of the Nature Society (Singapore) from 2000 to August 2008 and a Nominated Member of Parliament from 2005 to 2006.

Singapore's Garden City, conceived by the island-state's first Prime Minister (PM) Lee Kuan Yew, may not be original but was certainly remarkable, and even unique, for its time and place. That a tiny nascent developing country, suddenly stripped of its hinterland and whose survival was questionable, could see cleaning and greening as complementary to economic development was visionary. Equally remarkable was the thoroughness of its top-down planning and execution.

There was never any question that a clean and green Singapore was a pragmatic investment strategy "good for morale, for tourists and for investors" as once stated by PM Lee and would be a dramatic, visible manifestation of Singapore's inspiring rise from Third World to First.

The National Parks Board (NParks) is the government body entrusted with transforming this green vision into reality. Originally the Parks and Recreation Division,[1] it took on a new but important conservation role with its change of name and the introduction of the National Parks Act (1996). Since then the number of gazetted nature reserves has grown from one to four.[2]

Though its achievements are impressive, NParks is hampered by inadequate legislation, notably the lack of stipulation of the need for Environmental Impact Assessments (EIAs) before an area is redeveloped. Not only has this handicapped NParks in developing a more comprehensive and robust protection of our remaining natural heritage but it has pushed it into rearguard action in defending existing nature areas from incursions by other government agencies. Examples of unsustainable or paradoxical greening resulting from the lack of EIAs include the severing of Bukit Timah Nature Reserve, our remnant of primary forest, from the Central Catchment Area by an expressway, thus, compromising its long-term viability. People also question the rationale for the disproportionate number of golf courses in land-scarce Singapore — many abutting or even within nature area and reserves.[3]

[1] When its main role was providing parks and planting and maintaining roadside trees.

[2] Several reserves were degazetted between Independence and NParks inception.

[3] Twenty-three 18-hole and 15 nine-hole courses.

Also, NParks' restricted ambit in coastal conservation and the lack of any legal teeth in marine areas has resulted in there being no Marine Protected Areas (MPAs) despite our rich marine biodiversity while land reclamation at the iconic Tanjong Chek Jawa was reversed due to strong public, non-governmental organisation (NGO) and media action with NParks playing a back seat "advisory" role.

Realising its limited hard power and the unsustainability of a top-down approach, NParks has since been farsighted and effective in cultivating public support with a diverse array of outreach and education programmes. It also has strong working relationships of collaboration, complementarism and trust with local environmental non-governmental organisations (NGOs) such as the Nature Society (Singapore).

This enhancement of soft power has not only resulted in the physical greening of Singapore, but also a significant growth in the "green community".

NParks' sister organisation, Public Utilities Board (PUB), has followed suit and successfully launched their ABC Waters programme to develop and promote community ownership of our inland waterways and water bodies, critical for the supply and quality of our drinking water.

Unfortunately, National Environment Agency (NEA) which is responsible for urban cleaning has been less successful despite numerous valiant efforts. It would appear that nature areas inspire a greater sense of communal ownership than urban ones. Perhaps NEA could achieve more by promoting a deeper understanding of ecological principles. Their Singapore Green Plan, despite its name, is noticeably focused on "brown" issues and narrow efficiency targets rather than broader sustainability goals.

## Future Green Challenges

### Local

The greatest internal challenge to Singapore's greening and nature is demographic. The 2013 Population White Paper projected a population of 6.8 to 7 million by 2030 — a 25 percent growth in

15 years for what is already one of the densest cities in the world. A former chief planner had even stated publicly that doubling our population to 10 million is "doable".

"A Quality Living Environment" covers amenities such as transportation and includes accessibility to parks but there is no mention of nature areas.[4] There is also no evidence of analytical rigour in accessing social or environmental carrying capacity in these ambitious, economically-driven urban planning projections — hence, the demographic impact on Singapore's greenery is likely to be a "3-P Assault".

## Public Sector

Due to intense competition for land between different government agencies, the degradation, erosion and destruction of nature areas will certainly intensify with a growing population and agencies under pressure to acheive differing key performance indicators that seem to regard nature areas and even nature reserves as spare land "to be kept as long as is practical." While there is a growing awareness of our natural heritage among younger policy makers, the importance of ecosystem services will not be fully appreciated without mandatory Environmental Impact Assessments (EIAs).

## People Sector

The growing popularity of parks and nature amongst Singaporeans is evident and a recent survey actually showed that a majority (60 percent) wanted more greenery and less development.

However, unless our penchant for nature comes with a deeper understanding of human effects on the health of fragile ecosystems and a sense of responsibility to protect our nature areas, they are likely to be overwhelmed by a populace accustomed to a culture of consumption rather than conservation.

[4]Chapter 5 — Population White Paper: A Sustainable Population for a Dynamic Singapore.

NParks is faced with a dilemma as the number of visitors rather than biodiversity, was the yardstick by which its performance is gauged by policy makers. Universal education on the important differences in value between "man-made" green and natural ecosystems is essential. However, here too, NParks is faced with a Hobson's choice as the best education involves more exposure to nature areas and these are already overrun by the competing demands of various parts of the public sector and threatened by degradation from excessive human impact.

### Private Sector

Not surprisingly, the scarcity of land, the popularity of nature and the pragmatic approach of policy makers have already resulted in an increasing "commodification" of nature.

Private condominiums hug the boundary of our only primary forest and more are planned — built without EIAs or consultations with NParks. It appears that "nature at your doorstep" for a privileged few will result in less nature for the public.

Sentosa Island, originally touted as Singapore's playground, is now a playground for the global rich and famous with private condominiums and gated communities, casinos, hotels, marinas and golf clubs.

Spatial injustice whether real or perceived, can ignite smouldering resentment between the haves and have-nots as many recent examples globally have shown.

## Regional and Global Environmental Challenges

While our internal challenges seem daunting, they pale in comparison to external threats to our clean and green environment and future sustainability.

### Haze Pollution

The "Haze" is aptly named for an issue shrouded in smokescreens, layers of obfuscation and general lack of transparency. Initially blamed on "natural" forest fires, the smoke pollution from neighboring countries actually coincided with the massive land clearing and deforestation by multinational corporations (MNCs) involved in logging, pulp and paper production, and palm oil planting.[5] Global output of crude palm oil has been growing rapidly and the two largest producers, Indonesia and Malaysia, doubled the area for oil palm plantations between 1995 to 2005 alone to 10 million hectares. The forest and their biodiversity were victims, not culprits.

When the link was finally made, rounds of bilateral and regional talks and task forces were organised culminating in the milestone Transboundary Haze Pollution Agreement by ASEAN which Indonesia, the lynchpin, has yet to sign after 10 years. Instead various Indonesian ministers have defended its "right to develop" and even suggested that Singapore should "pay Indonesia for keeping her forests," if she wished to continue enjoying clean air.

The haze is a man-made problem driven by the profit motive. It is a classic illustration of how market fundamentalism ignores social and environmental externalities resulting in massive costs and serious consequences to the economy, society and the environment.[6]

A recent, notable trend is the outburst of criticism and complaints in social media directed at the Government for not doing more, by a Singapore public accustomed to clean air. It should be evident that there is very little Singapore can do as a government or even as a nation (despite our being the highest per capita consumer of paper and oil palm products in the region), unless the fundamental cause — market failure — is addressed and social and environmental costs are factored into the equation.

## Climate Change

A truly global problem in cause, distribution and effect and requiring solutions and cooperation on an unprecedented scale, climate

[5] Tropical forests do not naturally combust and spread like bush fires in drier countries.

[6] Estimated loss in 1997 for Singapore with health, tourism & airlines industries alone was S$97.5 to 110.5 million.

change is the ultimate complex environmental challenge that not only exacerbates all other environmental challenges but seriously affects global health, trade, security, the economy, and society in ways we are still struggling to comprehend. Its complexity is compounded by unpredictable timelines where the window of opportunity for effective action is small but the time lag between action and result is long.

How will Singapore face this challenge? Policy makers, while not unaware of the problem, seemed to put it on the back burner, at least publicly, until it appeared on the world economic stage. After that it was no longer credible for Singapore's reputation to underplay the issue or suppress our vulnerabilities as a small densely populated tropical island to the potential effects of rising temperatures and sea levels.

Our financial centre, petrochemical hub and important key industries, international airport, and many of our reservoirs and other essential amenities are set on coastal and/or on reclaimed land. The uncertain science of predicting rises in sea level may mean anything from expensive adaptation measures such as building sea walls and dikes or a catastrophic environmental disaster.

Singapore as a global city is also highly vulnerable to effects of climate change globally — from resource scarcity, pandemics to the opening of arctic trade route.

## Suggested Areas for Improvement

While prescriptive solutions for these challenges are beyond this chapter's ambit, some suggestions for enhancing Singapore's resilience and sustainability are proposed.

### Green Accounting

Singapore places considerable emphasis on numerical assessments such as rankings, performance indicators, and so on, not merely to indicate our competitiveness but as a guide to track progress and indicate areas for improvement.

However, while we have consistently punched above our weight on global economic competitiveness ratings, our performance in environmental rankings have been generally disappointing despite our clean and green image. Our response to these unfavourable rankings was to dismiss them as "irrelevant" or "unrepresentative" until the World Economic Forum published an Environmental Sustainability Index in which we ranked close to the bottom of the table. This prompted our Minister for Environment and Water Resources to register a formal objection and detailed explanation.

It is not surprising that although our economic competitiveness performance indicators compare us to other *countries*, our environmental indices are increasingly being compared with other cities, tacitly acknowledging our economic competitiveness but not our ecological sustainability.

While this may be a realistic representation of our strengths and weaknesses as a "city-state without a hinterland", it is not an honest appraisal of the fact that other cities have a hinterland and that Singapore, despite land constraints and the ingenious use of regional and even global hinterlands, cannot ignore the necessity for planning and locating key amenities such as our international airport and our water catchment areas within our own boundaries.

While environmental sustainability rankings may be like comparing apples with oranges, their components provide valuable data and information which would be dangerous for us to marginalise, alter or ignore. We have already seen how the lack of EIAs has compromised our environmental planning in areas such as flood control and climate change adaptation.

Beyond depriving ourselves of critical information, we are also failing to develop the capacity to collect, analyse and interpret this information. Importing this expertise is not a viable alternative as much of it is highly location-specific. For the same reason, sending Singaporeans abroad to learn may only work in a limited context and the real lessons have to be learnt at home instead.

More regional and international disputes will also be about environmental issues and it is important for us to have the wherewithal to represent ourselves and defend our rights in these areas.

In an increasingly complex and chaotic world filled with environmental challenges, all information is important, especially those that highlight our weaknesses. We have achieved economic success through objective appraisal, honest evaluation and analytical rigour in order to formulate the correct policies. Our precarious dependency on water has also been met with the same approach and determination to overcome the odds. We need to extend, broaden and apply this approach to environmental sustainability.

## Learning from Mother Nature

Good ecological data may provide the essential stepping-stones or alphabet to meet future environmental challenges but we also need insight and expertise to join the dots or read the text.

The extreme complexity of life sciences and biodiversity has made deciphering, formulating, comprehending and quantifying them far more challenging than the hard or mathematical sciences; However, the inability to read the language is not a reason to destroy the literature. Innumerable scientists, polymaths and thought leaders from Sir Francis Bacon to Richard Feynman and from Leonardo to da Vinci to Nassim Taleb, have emphasised the importance of respecting and "learning from Mother Nature, the oldest and wisest".

Despite or perhaps even because of our Garden City, many Singaporeans including policy makers have an inverted, limited and overly utilitarian concept of our natural environment.

"Nature in its original and authentic form and in its claim to space appears to have little place in the physical development of the City-state. Nature where it can be managed and located to fit into overall land use development schemes seems much preferred..." (Oei). This excessively narrow anthropocentric perspective is also mirrored in our promotion of 'life sciences' up till recently.

Understandably, Singapore size, constraints and limited resources require us to carefully select and focus on areas in which to excel but this should not result in a corresponding shrinkage of our knowledge base. This tunnel vision has already restricted our ability to formulate sustainable environment policies and it will be a serious handicap in an even more challenging future.

Many of the advantages of developing an "Ecological Quotient" such as intellectual curiosity, innovative thinking and emotional resilience are difficult to prove and almost impossible to quantify. But "ecological" thinking translated to biomimicry, green technology, nature-based solutions and the optimisation of ecosystem services are rapidly growing fields of endeavor and while putting a monetary figure to them is often easier after the damage is done (e.g. the haze, floods, oils spills and other man-made environmental disasters), there are inspiring examples of the ecosystem approach to sustainability incorporating the preventive principle. Two iconic ideas that involve water management are: first, New York City's investment of $1 billion in purchasing and improving watershed forests and soil around its reservoirs. By reducing pollution and conserving water, these forests enhanced both the quantity and quality of New York's water and also avoided a $60 billion purchase of a state-of-the-art filtration plant (excluding running costs). Second, Dutch engineers employing not just expensive pumps but also planting trees (whose roots can take in 80 gallons a day each) to maintain drainage and reduce flooding in reclaimed land in Holland.

Singapore should not neglect the forest-water nexus when trying to solve our flooding issues rather than focus on massive and expensive engineering works involving a high underground water-holding area that NEA has indicated will "take at least 10 years to show results."

## Green Global Positioning

Singapore's performance abroad has been as stellar as that at home and "a new state without a hinterland has succeeded in making a hinterland of the global economy with conspicuous success" (Leifer). Notwithstanding this, Singapore's leaders are constantly mindful of the city-state's vulnerabilities and vigilant in identifying potential threats to our survival.

They have assiduously constructed a strong web of multilateral diplomatic, economic, trade, security and institutional relationships, both as a network for advancement and as a safety net.

Singapore upholds the rule of law and supports good global governance as a credible, responsible and proactive global citizen (while maintaining its sovereign rights). Above all, the nation strives to remain connected, useful and relevant to the global community.

However, in the face of looming global environmental challenges, weak areas and gaps have appeared and while creating a global hinterland for economic growth has paid rich dividends, they now expose the city-state to greater environmental vulnerabilities which may undermine its economic success.

Singapore's green global presence has not been negligible though less spectacular than her economic success. The city-state has actively participated in international environmental conferences such as the Earth Summit where it played a prominent role. It has also donated generously to disaster relief in both funds and manpower. It has also not been slow in exporting its clean and green image, urban "Garden City" planning and more recently, its successful water technology.

However, critics of Singapore's green model point to the unsustainability of its consumption patterns, the size of its per capita ecological footprint (5.3 earths) and its carbon-intensive growth. Its predilection for expensive technological solutions rather than conservation and a stronger 3R culture, its preference for "weak" rather than "deep" green solutions, its lack of mandatory EIAs despite being a signatory of Convention on International Trade in Endangered Species (CITES) and, perhaps most disturbingly, a growing tendency to defend, promote, and market the Singapore model rather than learn from others' best practices.

The Sino-Singapore Tianjin Eco-City project, promoted as "China's national green development zone" and modelled on Singapore's policies and expertise, has reportedly found the Chinese setting more stringent standards and broader targets than Singapore had to offer.

Singapore needs to develop greater ecological rigour and a more sustainable environmental perspective to its greening both at home and abroad in order to remain relevant and credible. Otherwise, in today's world of flux, the kaleidoscope may suddenly shift and our international standing may change from one of economic high-flyer to environmental freeloaders.

## Conclusion

Singapore's policy makers have always prided themselves on seeing the big picture and taking a long term view but the lens they have used is primarily economic and even our greening has been narrowly utilitarian and equally shortsighted in focus.

In a future of complex environmental challenges, many of them global, it is critical that we do not view the economy and the environment as a balancing act or even a triple bottomline.

The big picture is the natural environment which encompasses and provides the life-support system for people and the economy. Failure to see this was possible in the past when the pressure was smaller but the exponential growth of both is increasingly pushing our environmental envelope.

It is essential we see the world through an ecological lens and make policies accordingly if we wish to ensure our future sustainability.

# Chapter 9

# Singapore Challenged: The Natural and Living Environment*

*Euston Quah and Christabelle Soh*

* This article was originally published in Commentary: Volume 23 titled "Singapore Challenged: The Uneasy and Unchartered Road Ahead" © 2014 The National University of Singapore Society. Dr Euston Quah is Albert Winsemius Chair Professor of Economics and Director of the Economic Growth Centre at Nanyang Technological University (NTU), Singapore. He is also editor of the *Singapore Economic Review* and president of the Economic Society of Singapore. At the time of writing, Christabelle Soh was an economics teacher at Raffles Institution. She is a recipient of the Lee Kuan Yew Gold Medal for Economics (NTU) in 2010.

## Introduction

The study of Economics revolves around the fundamental problem of scarcity. In the face of limited resources and unlimited wants, how can any society be organised to ensure that resources are allocated to the right areas? The trade-offs involved in the choices made and the resulting conflicts in objectives present a challenge to all governments. With respect to Singapore, the most pertinent challenge stems from managing higher economic growth and the need to balance that with conserving and protecting the environment (broadly defined as comprising the living and natural environment). While all countries face this challenge, Singapore's circumstances make the trade-offs especially stark.

On one hand, globalisation and the associated reduction in barriers to trade and capital flows have facilitated the rise of regional economic rivals. Singapore's export- and foreign direct investment-led growth model is under threat from countries such as China, which have the advantage of cheap and abundant labour to create both export competitiveness while attracting foreign domestic investment (FDI). While this only poses a problem for Singapore to the extent that such countries export similar goods and services and attract similar types of FDI to Singapore, the fact that these regional countries are currently looking to move up the value chain means that the scenario of Singapore and them being in direct competition may not be far into the distant future. The implication is that to achieve the same degree of economic growth, Singapore needs to be more competitive than ever. The increased competition from rival economies has caused the trade-off in terms of pursuing higher economic growth vis-a-vis protection and conserving the natural environment while raising the non-material aspects of quality of life. With higher incomes and the satisfaction of material needs, people start demanding cleaner air and water, larger green open spaces, more recreation and leisure time, increased spaces for reflection, conservation of heritage, the arts and culture and so on.

The theory is similar to that which underpins the environmental Kuznets curve, an n-shaped curve that describes the relationship between growth/income and the degree of pollution over time. Beyond a certain level of income, the demands for a cleaner environment would lead to less pollution and hence, a reduction in pollution as income increases. Similarly, beyond a certain level of income, people are less willing to trade aspects of non-material welfare for more material aspects of growth.

To sustain economic growth in the face of increased foreign competition, aspects of non-material welfare may need to be sacrificed. However, at the same time, Singaporeans' demands for improvement in the quality of life have increased. Managing both sides and striking an appropriate balance forms the broad, fundamental challenge Singapore faces today.

## Trade-offs between Economic Growth and the Environment

### The Energy Challenge

Economic growth entails greater production (and consumption) of goods and services. This inevitably involves higher levels of energy consumption. How best to meet this increased energy demand is a specific challenge that Singapore faces.

Singapore currently relies primarily on burning fossil fuels to generate energy. There are two issues with this approach. Firstly, relying on conventional sources of energy from burning fossil fuels results in higher carbon emissions. Although Singapore only contributes to 0.2 percent of global carbon emissions, we have always punched above our weight in global affairs and should also do so with regard to setting an example in reducing carbon emissions. While Singapore has done well in this area, achieving one of the lowest carbon intensities (kilogrammes of carbon dioxide emissions per dollar gross domestic product (GDP)) in the world, the challenge lies in further decoupling growth and carbon emissions. This requires even further reductions in carbon intensity, which may prove to be costly. The main factor behind our low carbon intensity is the fuel makeup in our energy production. Since 2000, we have increased the use of natural gas, the least carbon-emitting fossil fuel, from 19 percent to 80 percent of the total fuel mix.[1] Increasing the share of natural gas is the low-hanging fruit. Given the high proportion of natural gas in the fuel mix, there is little scope for further reductions in carbon intensity from this source. Further reductions in carbon intensity may require costly technology such as carbon capture and storage. This leads us to the second issue of cost. To maintain competitiveness, Singapore needs to keep energy costs low. If cost were the only consideration, coal would definitely be the fuel of choice, especially when countries such as China have an abundance of it and hence, a cost advantage stemming from lower energy costs. However, coal emits the most carbon dioxide when burnt and is the most pollutive of the fossil fuels. Again, the pressure to remain competitive and environmental considerations pull in different directions.

The problem is compounded by the fact that Singapore is renewable energy-deficient. Renewable energy could potentially provide a way out of the conundrum since it does not produce any carbon emission. However, Singapore is not blessed with the ability to rely on these renewable sources. We lack the land mass for wind turbines and fast flowing rivers for hydroelectricity. Solar energy is still too costly and faces the issue of storage to allow the timing of energy production to match that of consumption. Furthermore, we lack sufficient space for the buffer zone which a nuclear energy plant would require.

In view of these considerations, the challenge is two-fold. In the short run, we need to decide on an optimal energy mix that strikes a balance between cost and environmental concerns. In the longer term, the focus should be minimising the trade-off between the two. On the supply-side, we need to continually explore and develop less carbon intensive energy sources. On the demand side, we will need to manage energy demand from both households and industry. Naturally, this is easier said than done. Energy needs to be cheap, clean, and secure. The road forward is continued monitoring and

[1] National Climate Change Secretariat, http://app.nccs.gov.sg/page.aspx?pageid=167&secid=193.

pursuit of energy efficiency, research and development on clean energy including how to make coal usage cleaner, and energy security by diversifying the sources of energy (which raises another difficulty and often costly trade-off between reliance on a narrow range of traditional supply vis-a-vis searching for alternative sources). The cheapest and easiest way is to develop a shared smart grid involving supplies from regional countries which already have an abundance of natural renewable energy resources. But, this again raises the problem of energy security where the source is not in Singapore's determination. On the demand side, it is also very important that both consumers and producers are responsive in their behaviours towards the usage of energy. This requires a good understanding and application of behavioural economics. There is only so much that legislated economic incentives can do to affect behaviour. Behavioural nudges are needed to complement the conventional economic incentives.

## The Population Challenge

The long run economic growth rate is dependent on the productive capacity of an economy. Singapore's ageing population means that all else being constant, economic growth will slow down and may even turn negative. An ageing population means that entrants into the labour force will be outnumbered by retirees from the labour force. This would cause a shrinkage of the labour force and hence, a reduction in productive capacity and growth. According to the Government's 2013 Population White Paper, in the absence of foreign labour inflows, Singapore's population (and hence, labour force) would start shrinking in 2025.[2] In the absence of productivity gains, continued economic growth would require growing labour force. However, Singapore's low fertility rate means that it is not viable to depend on the labour force to increase via domestic means.

---

[2] National Population and Talent Division, *A Sustainable Population for a Dynamic Singapore*, http://population.sg/whitepaper/resource-files/population-white-paper.pdf.

The labour force requires foreign augmentation. This, unfortunately, has come with a trade-off in terms overcrowding and a reduction in the quality of life due to congestion on public transport networks and a strain on the social fabric.

While improvements in productivity have been trumpeted as the cure, there are good reasons to doubt the viability of the productivity targets over the next decade. Firstly, large gains in productivity are usually only enjoyed by developing countries which are playing catch-up. This is because there are still many low-hanging fruits in the form of best practices and existing technology that they can adopt. Singapore does not fall into this category. We have plucked most of the low-hanging fruit and there is no longer a technological gap between us and the rest of the developed world. Secondly, the rough empirics do not add up. The most dynamic economy in the world is arguably the United States, which only saw an increase in productivity of 1.7 percent over the past decade. For Singapore, greater gains in productivity will require an even higher level of dynamism which is unlikely to be realised within a decade. Thirdly, while there are specific industries which have significant room for improvement in productivity (e.g. construction), the scope for improvement in the overall economy's productivity depends on the future relative sizes of these industries as well. It is quite likely that Singapore will not experience significant improvements in productivity and will miss the ambitious productivity targets of 2 to 3 percent annual growth in productivity over the 2010 to 2020 decade.[3]

The implication of the above is that the trade-off between growth and overcrowding is going to remain tight for the foreseeable future. Where there are trade-offs, there must exist an optimal point where the marginal benefits of an addition to the population (in the form of a larger labour force and growth) is equivalent to the marginal cost (in the form of the contribution to overcrowding).[4]

---

[3]Economic Strategies Committee, *Report of the Economic Strategies Committee: High-skilled People, Innovative Economy, Distinctive Global City*, http://app.mof.gov.sg/data/cmsresource/ESC%20Report/ESC%20Full%20Report.pdf.

[4]Quah, Euston, and Soh, Christabelle "Optimal population: Why non-material welfare matters," November 17, 2012.

The challenge then, for the short term, is to find that optimal population size and to adjust the foreign labour flows to reach it. For the longer term, the focus on productivity is still appropriate and necessary. Long-run solutions should, in general, try to minimise the trade off costs instead of simply managing the trade-off. Improvements in productivity raises the productive capacity without the need to import foreign labour and avoids the sacrifice of non-material well-being.

## The Waste Challenge

Both energy and population present challenges because they are ingredients necessary for economic growth. Waste, on the other hand, presents a challenge because it is a by-product of growth. With growth, there is greater output and consumption — both contribute to waste. Between 2000 and 2012, in line with the increase in national income, waste generated (in tonnes) increased by 56 percent.[5]

Singapore's current waste management system primarily involves incineration and the use of landfills. Both involve trade-offs in the form of a worsened living environment. The former causes air pollution and poorer air quality. It also adds to Singapore's carbon emissions. The latter causes land and possibly, groundwater pollution. Furthermore, with land becoming increasingly scarce, the opportunity cost of landfills in the form of foregone development projects become ever larger. The problem is compounded by the fact that the Pulau Semakau landfill site is expected to reach its capacity in 2016. Current efforts to expand the site are projected to extend this to 2035.[6] However, despite the National Environment Agency's best efforts, there will inevitably be some negative impact on the marine life nearby.

---

[5] "Singapore Waste Statistics 2012," ZeroWasteSg, http://www.zerowastesg.com/tag/recycling-rate/.

[6] "NEA plan seeks to limit damage from landfill expansion," *The Straits Times*, August 23, 2013.

There is a need to reduce the amount of waste generated. One way to generate less waste is by accepting less growth. The challenge is to find out how much growth and consumption Singaporeans are willing to give up to enjoy a low-waste and cleaner environment and implementing a suitable tax to discourage consumption. The other way to generate less waste is to decouple growth from waste generation — in other words, recycle. Recycling allows increased production and consumption without a corresponding increase in resource usage and thereby waste generation. In this regard, Singapore has thus far produced a mixed bag of results. While 60 percent of total waste is recycled, a breakdown of the recycling rates by materials reveals that the bulk of the recycling is carried out by the industrial sector. Recycling rates of materials more associated with household use (e.g. plastics) are dismally low.[7] The challenge then is to change households' attitudes and encourage greater household recycling. However, recycling itself is not a panacea. Recycling waste without increasing demand for the recycled products will not be sustainable. This subsequently often requires huge subsidies which compete with subsidies provided to incineration plants. Furthermore, if waste reduction were successful, there would be less waste produced for recycling which in turn, will threaten recycling firms. What is needed is a holistic evaluation of the entire waste problem from its inception and generation to a cost-benefit analysis of each proposed solution. The cheapest and most efficient way to dispose non-toxic waste is to lease waste landfill sites outside of Singapore. However, this again is politically not suitable despite its economic appeal. Nonetheless, there have been success stories in the various import-export waste states in the United States and this perhaps, bears studying.

## Addressing the Challenges

Long-term solutions to all three challenges mentioned above require delinking growth from the problems' sources — carbon

---

[7]"Waste Statistics and Recycling Rate for 2012," NEA, http://app2.nea.gov.sg/energy-waste/waste-management/waste-statistics-and-overall-recycling.

emissions, increases in population, and waste generation. These will involve new technology, new means of doing things or fundamental changes in attitudes. These are big ideas and involve a certain degree of uncertainty. While important, they provide little by way of concrete and immediate steps that can be taken.

For a more immediate response, the focus is to manage the challenges. This involves accepting the trade-offs as a given and finding out what the optimal compromise is. Fundamentally, it is an exercise in optimisation. What amount of growth and the corresponding levels of carbon emissions, foreign labour, and waste would maximise social welfare? Would an additional percentage increase in real GDP bring about greater social utility? This requires greater and more consistent use of cost-benefit analysis. While the Ministry of Finance has taken steps in the right direction in adopting more consistent use of cost-benefit analyses, what Singapore still lacks is a systematic gathering of data regarding non-market goods such as green spaces and fresh air. More valuation studies need to be carried out to derive society's preferences in order to determine what the optimal trade-offs are. Economics provides many tools to place monetary values on these non-material aspects of welfare. It is easy to use these tools to aid enlightened policymaking. Additionally, the act of soliciting society's preferences has the benefit of more visible involvement of stakeholders, more transparency in decision choices, and better informed decision-making.

## Conclusion

In summary, Singapore's challenges primarily stem from the trade-off between economic growth and other objectives. While globalisation and greater competition have meant that each unit of growth will require greater sacrifice, increased affluence have pulled in the opposite direction with greater demand for a higher quality of life. To address these challenges, long run solutions must involve reducing the trade-offs. Concrete steps however, require short run management. This involves finding an optimal balance, which in turn requires a systematic collection of new and relevant data.

A step that Singapore could take is to set up an agency to conduct and update valuation studies regarding non-market goods and accounting for non-material aspects of growth. This agency would greatly complement what is now increasingly demanded of cost-benefit studies on project proposals and will serve Singapore well into the future by continually inferring and analysing society's preferences.

This article was written from the conventional perspective of growth as the main objective and the resultant trade-offs as necessary evils. However, a paradigm shift might be in order. It might be preferable to redefine the objective of policies to one that pursues higher quality of life of which the focus is on the non-material aspects of life. Here, growth is but a means to an end. This will require a new mindset which re-estimates the optimal population, energy source, and waste management system — not from how they support growth, but from how they affect a defined quality of life. This may be the real challenge instead.

# Chapter 10

# Iron Trees and Cheap Water: Environmental Identities in Singapore*

*Leong Ching*

* This article was originally published in Commentary, Volume 27 titled "SGP4.0: An Agenda" © 2018 The National University of Singapore Society. Dr Leong Ching is Vice Provost (Student Life) and Associate Professor at the Lee Kuan Yee School of Public Policy, National University of Singapore.

Much of Singapore's national identity has been shaped by its size and geography. The fact that it is a city-state forms the exoskeleton of the national narrative — the smallness of our market requiring openness and economic porosity; our vulnerability necessitating nimbleness in foreign affairs.

But, as the biophysical and planetary limitations for growth are reached and, increasingly, breached in many parts of the world, environmental issues have acquired new salience in Singapore.

The environment has all too often been the final item on any national policy agenda but may now become a far more salient one that our country's fourth generation (4G) leaders and indeed all of us will have to grapple with.

## Emergence of an Identity Shaped by Environmental Insecurities: Anthropocentrity

To interrogate the idea of "the environment" within Singapore, it helps to understand the concept of "environmental identity". It defines the relationship between people and their natural environment. Such an identity carries not just emotional significance, but normative and prescriptive value too.

Like all identities, an environmental identity is constituted by a variety of factors and is closely linked not only to individual perception, but to social and cultural narratives, as well as public and political institutions. Environmental identity is, therefore, a composite of perceptions, shared history and beliefs, all of which inform the choices we make and the way we behave.

One way of thinking about environmental identity is along the ecocentric-anthropocentric scales created by Thompson and Barton that evaluate people's attitudes towards the environment, and their levels of support for environmental issues.[1]

Ecocentric individuals find inherent value in nature, believing that nature is worthy of preservation for its own sake. On the other

---

[1] Thomson, Suzanne C. Gagnon, and Barton, Michelle A., "Ecocentric and Anthropocentric Attitudes Toward the Environment," *Journal of Environmental Psychology* 14, no. 2 (June 1994), 149–157.

hand, anthropocentric individuals take an instrumental view where nature is treated as the means by which human comfort and quality of life may be extracted and maintained.

Not surprisingly, those living in a bustling city-state like Singapore are more likely to be anthropocentric.

Since our independence in 1965, the Singaporean national narrative has revolved around the concept of vulnerability. Singapore's split from neighbouring Malaysia left it bereft, with "no hinterland, no natural resources, and almost total dependence on Malaysia for water supplies" as it is often said.

The resulting sense of vulnerability — as much constructed as real — was regularly affirmed by political leaders and foreign observers. Founding Prime Minister, Lee Kuan Yew once described it as an "inescapable, permanent condition of Singapore as an independent republic".[2]

This is particularly pronounced when it comes to the issue of food and water insecurity. Water, repeatedly called an "existential issue" for Singaporeans, has also been a perennial source of tension in the country's relations with Malaysia, upon which we depend for water.

In 1961 and 1962, Singapore signed two separate water agreements with Malaysia that would allow it to draw water from Johor and the Johor River. These would expire in 2011 and 2061 respectively. Since then, several talks attempting to revise or establish fresh agreements have stalled, with Malaysian leaders periodically threatening to cut off Singapore's water supply.

Kog *et al.* termed this the practice of *hydropolitik,* or the political exploitation of a "life-and-death gambit" of a resource which is frequently described as a matter of national security.[3]

---

[2] Heng, Yee-Kuang, "A Global City in an Age of Global Risks: Singapore's Evolving Discourse on Vulnerability," *Contemporary Southeast Asia* 35, no. 3 (December 2013), 423–446.

[3] Kog, Yue Choong, Lim, Irvin Fang Jau, and Long, Joey Shi Ruey, *Beyond Vulnerability?: Water in Singapore-Malaysia Relations* (RSIS Monograph No. 3) (Singapore: Institute of Defence and Strategic Studies, 2002).

To minimise this, Singapore's Public Utilities Board (PUB) introduced the "Four National Taps" water management strategy to expand the sources of water — from imported water and water from local catchments to include desalination and recycled wastewater (also known as NEWater). The goal is to move towards achieving complete self-sufficiency in water by 2060.

While Singapore's initial intention was to address those "life and death" challenges in securing water supplies, it is now building a global hydrohub identity based on its strength in water policies and is sharing its experiences with an international community that is increasingly burdened by environmental and climate challenges.

What was once an inescapable fact has now been eroded by technology and policy. In the late 1990s, when Malaysia mooted the idea of revising the water prices, the key element was that there was only one seller; Singapore was a price-taker. Today, with desalination and recycling, the equation has shifted. True, there is only one seller, but there really is only one buyer. This leads to a new environmental identity around water — one that includes confidence that Singapore no longer has to bend its knee in future water talks with Malaysia.

The same narrative applies to food. While Singapore produces about 10 percent of its total consumption of food, it is the third most food secure country in the world.[4] This is because food security is measured not by the actual amount of food produced, but by the exposure a country has to any single food source — Singapore imports from diverse sources. This sense of security perversely means that, on average, each Singaporean household throws out 2.5kg of food waste, which is the equivalent of a bag of rice, each week.[5]

Overall, while the current situation of relative food and water security may seem to portend a safe and stable situation for the country, it also means our view of natural resources such as water and food is highly anthropocentric. This in turn will impact our

[4] Ong, Keng Yong, "Singapore and Food Security," *RSIS Commentary*, June 30, 2017, http://hdl.handle.net/11540/7233.

[5] "2.5kg of food a week wasted by each household, equal to half of all household waste: NEA study," *The Straits Times*, December 3, 2017.

behaviour and hence our resilience to environmental changes and climatic events.

## An Artifice of Nature: Resilience and Behaviour

A more fundamental question therefore is this: What is the Singaporean conception of "nature"? When so much of "nature" is in fact man-made — from manicured parks to reclaimed land — how do Singaporeans understand "nature" and how do we derive our environmental identity?

The artificial and the natural are frequently thought of as polarities, but in the case of Singapore, the relationship is more complex. The best way to illustrate this is to take the example of Singapore's Urban Beautification Programme, launched in 1967 which is overseen by a "Garden City Action Committee" comprising senior civil servants.

The Government announced its plan to build a "Garden City", planted trees along major roads, and creepers and climbers to camouflage concrete structures such as flyovers and over-head bridges. Angsana trees — "instant trees" — were imported and planted along public roads and streets, sometimes even before construction is completed.

More recently, the "ABC Waters" (Active, Beautiful, Clean) programme which won the international Waterfront Awards in its year of completion (2012), saw an investment of S$76.7 million to turn concrete canals into meandering rivers, transforming Singapore into a "City of Gardens and Water".

Which is more natural? A city with concrete buildings and highways, or one with instant trees and creeper covers? A plain, utilitarian canal, or one that has been turned into a "river" quite unlike the original? The "natural" in Singapore contrasts with the more obviously artificial, but is no less man-made.

"Nature" in Singapore is not feral but constructed, as Barnard argues.[6] The Singapore Government took its technocratic, managerial approach to economic development and transferred it

[6] Barnard, Timothy P., *Nature Contained: Environmental Histories of Singapore* (Singapore: NUS Press, 2014).

to the "Garden City" project to cultivate a form of greenery which is tamed to fit with its idea of urban development.

Lee Kuan Yew said at the opening of the National Orchid Garden in 1995:

> Singapore today is a verdant city, where abundant greenery softens the landscape. This was no accident of nature. It is the result of a deliberate 30-year policy, which required political will and sustained effort to carry out.[7]

Hence, the artificial-natural dichotomy is by no means unproblematic. Groups such as the Nature Society, for example, argue that nature has become a "human construct" in Singapore, and greening for aesthetic purposes has come at the expense of encouraging robust natural vegetative growth and biodiversity. The most visible symbol of this is at Gardens by the Bay, where the defining features are its "iron trees".

It may be unsurprising for a dense city-state to have an artificial sense of what comprises the natural environment. But environmental identities have implications on our behaviour today as well as the ability to adapt in the future.

## Resilience

A consistent thread in the agenda of the 4G political leaders is building national resilience which is the psychological ability to withstand shocks and challenges. Within environmental sciences, resilience is commonly defined as a system's ability to resist change and withstand external disturbances.[8]

---

[7] "A Special Tribute to Mr Lee Kuan Yew, The Man Behind the Greening of Singapore," National Parks Board, https://www.nparks.gov.sg/about-us/special-tribute-to-mr-lee.

[8] Holling, C.S., "Resilience and Stability of Ecological Systems," http://www.zoology.ubc.ca/bdg/pdfs_bdg/2013/Holling%201973.pdf.

Resilience takes on two broad forms in addressing the different types of risk that surface. The first is defined by a "status quo bias" of maintaining the same relationships and resisting external change.

The second conception of resilience is defined not by the system's ability to build up a bulwark against change but instead to the ability to adapt and adjust to fluctuations. This emphasises elasticity and flexibility in the face of change. These two forms of resilience impact the way that environmental identity may be expressed.

In the first view, pro-environmental behaviour is primarily expressed in the provision and strengthening of large-scale human-built infrastructure to guard against further environmental degradation and climate change. This is evidenced in the building of dams, dykes, and seawalls.

In the second view, pro-environmental behaviour is expressed through adaptive human behavioural change, and the cultivation and maintenance of ecosystems, of which humans are a part. This entails the building of institutional capacity and communities, as well as the introduction of incentives to change the way resources are allocated.

## Emerging Climate Change Elements within the National Environmental Identity

In 2012, Singapore recorded the highest carbon footprint among Asia-Pacific countries; in 2014, we recorded the seventh-largest ecological footprint out of 150 countries. How do Singaporeans feel about our environmental record?

In a survey conducted by Singapore's National Climate Change Secretariat in 2013, it was found that 70.2 percent of Singaporeans were concerned about climate change, and 78.5 percent believed that they would be adversely affected it.

However, when it came to personal responsibility, only 39.2 percent felt that individuals were responsible for taking action, while a larger proportion felt that it was up to the Government, businesses, or non-government organisations to do so.[9] This shows that while Singaporeans are certainly aware of the threat of climate change, a majority do not feel personally culpable or moved to take action.

A good example is when Singapore experienced a two-month drought in 2014 with February that year being the driest month since 1869. There was near-zero rainfall. Facing similar circumstances, neighbouring Malaysia implemented water rationing in Johor, Selangor, Negeri Sembilan, as well as the Federal Territories of Kuala Lumpur and Putrajaya. In Thailand, 20 provinces were declared drought-disaster areas. It was business as usual in Singapore. Water consumption advisories were sent only to commercial and industrial users.[10] There was no water rationing.[11]

The implication is that even in the face of severe climatic change, it is likely that Singaporeans will find it hard to change their behaviour. At the same time, extreme weather events including heavy rainfall and exceptionally dry periods are projected to occur more frequently in the region as a whole.

The crucial issue behind this attitude lies in our environmental identity. What do people think about the possibility of drought? What do they think they should do about it? What do they think the Government should do about it?

---

[9] *Climate Change Public Perception Survey*, National Climate Change Secretariat, https://www.nccs.gov.sg/docs/default-source/default-document-library/appendix-i.pdf.

[10] "Singapore experiencing record dry spell — and it could get worse: NEA," *The Straits Times*, February 25, 2014. Also: "Singapore endures driest month since 1869," *TODAY Online*, March 4, 2014, https://www.todayonline.com/singapore/singapore-endures-driest-month-1869. Also, Zulkifli, Masagos, speech at Budget Debate, March 1, 2017, https://www.mewr.gov.sg/news/speech-by-mr-masagos—zulkifli-minister-for-the-environment-and-water-resources-during-budget-debates—1-mar-2017.

[11] Leong, Ching, "Resilience to Climate Change Events: The Paradox of Water (In)-security," *Sustainable Cities and Society* 27 (2016): 439–447.

Recently, the PUB also announced it would raise water tariffs by 30 percent (to be spread over two years) for the first time in 20 years, in an effort to curb the excessive consumption of water. Even as laws, regulations, and economic incentives may result in temporary behavioural changes, they may not be able to change attitudes in any lasting or permanent way. As such, the ultimate aim of demand-side management ought to be to educate and engage the public to help it relate to climate change on a more personal level.

Much of Singapore's national policymaking has been guided by economic pragmatism and anxiety about the future, but such a mode of decision-making is often at odds with the public good of fostering environmentally-sustainable behaviour. When it comes to the environment, as with many other common pool resources, beneficiaries do not want to incur the costs required to sustain the environment, or are powerless to enforce the levying of costs on those who extract these environmental assets.

In short, all three emerging elements of the Singaporean environmental identity present challenges to the 4G leaders if they wish to shift policy towards greater environmental sustainability. These are first, an anthropocentric attitude that does not see the intrinsic value of the natural environment but believes that nature is malleable to human will; second, excessive carbon emissions that will invariably impede Singapore's quality of life in years to come; third, and concurrently, Singapore's reliance on infrastructure and government policies when it comes to tackling critical climate change issues, instead of adopting strategies of social adaptation and behavioural change.

An anthropocentric attitude towards its environmental assets is a part of the environmental identity of the Singaporean and cannot be easily moved. Yet, within the arc of development in Singapore, the economic pragmatism that has bred this very identity can be used to serve an environmental goal — perhaps one way of reversing the overuse of our environmental resources is to see the importance of the environment in sustaining economic life itself.

# Population

# Chapter 11

# Reflections on Singapore's Demographic Future*

*Paul Cheung*

*This article was originally published in Commentary: Volume 23 titled "Singapore Challenged: The Uneasy and Unchartered Road Ahead" © 2014 The National University of Singapore Society. Dr Paul Cheung is a Professor (Practice) at the Lee Kuan Yew School of Public Policy, National University of Singapore, and Director of the Asia Competitiveness Institute at the School. He was director of Population Planning Unit of Singapore Government from 1986 to 1995 and Singapore's Chief Statistician from 1991 to 2004.

In 1986, Dr Kwa Soon Bee, then Permanent Secretary of the Ministry of Health (MOH), asked to see me in his office. It was a cordial meeting and we discussed a range of population and public health issues. A few days later, I was asked whether I would like to join the MOH and to help establish the Population Planning Unit (PPU). Having just started my teaching career at the University of Singapore after six years of post-graduate training in demography and social planning, I was hesitant. Eventually, I was persuaded and began a joint appointment at the MOH as Director of Population Planning Unit (PPU). My first task was to help formulate the "New Population Policy" which was announced in 1987 by Mr Goh Chok Tong, then Deputy Prime Minister (DPM), to replace the "Stop at Two" policy. Since then, I have been a keen observer of Singapore's demographic trends and helped shape some of its population policies.

Population policy in 2013 has once again become a hot political issue. A wide range of views has been expressed on the desired population size, the number of migrant workers and many critical (and sometimes cynical) comments have been expressed in social media. Critics have faulted the Government for pushing for a larger population and, more importantly, for neglecting the citizen base in favour of the foreigners.

This debate on our population policy is necessary and desirable, as we need to articulate a common future. At each debate, we have become clearer in our understanding of Singaporean society, with the Government adjusting its policy stance correspondingly.

During the 1987 debate, the need for the Government to address issues related to the costs of childbearing and raising a family was brought home. The policy package thus focused specifically on reducing the cost of bringing up a family. Subsequent policy revisions in 2006 helped reduce these burdens further. The current debate has already led to revisions in our manpower policies and we can probably expect more refinements to our immigration policies in the near future.

As I reflect on the current debate on population size and the critical comments that have been expressed, I see the need to once again revisit the demographic challenges facing Singapore and assess our scientific understanding of Singapore's population dynamics as the basis for our projections and population policy recommendations. Why do we now project a population of 6.9 million when not too long ago we said four million would be ideal? Did we make a mistake in our calculations? If we are on track in our technical assessment of our population dynamics, what then is our demographic future? How should we as citizens of this city-state face up to the demographic challenge? I share some of my reflections here.

## A Deteriorating Age Structure

Singapore has a strong registration system for births and deaths and our demographic information system is among the best in the world. A solid information base thus facilitates our understanding of the changing age structure. We have been tracking the changing age structure of residents over time. In the 1980s, when I started work at the PPU, we knew that we were entering into a period of "high demographic dividend", i.e. the dependency ratio was at its lowest due to the much larger working age population relative to the "dependent" younger and older populations. In the 1980s, the index of dependency ratio was about 46 to 100, which marked the beginning of this "dividend" period. Figure 1 shows vividly the trough period and the impending surge in the dependency ratio.

We know for a fact that the future rise of the dependency ratio is entirely due to the increase in older persons, especially those from the baby boom cohorts. We have been tracking the movement of the baby boom cohorts for many years. There is no escape from this "silver tsunami". The size of the ageing baby boomers will make their presence felt in many aspects: the demand for health care, the management of their daily lives, the end-of-life issues, and the impact arising from the inter-generational transfer of assets. We are also aware that, with the rising life expectancy (from 72 years in 1980 to 82 in 2012), older persons will live and stay healthy for much longer. At age 60, a Singaporean male can expect to live another 23 years and a Singaporean female, 26 years.

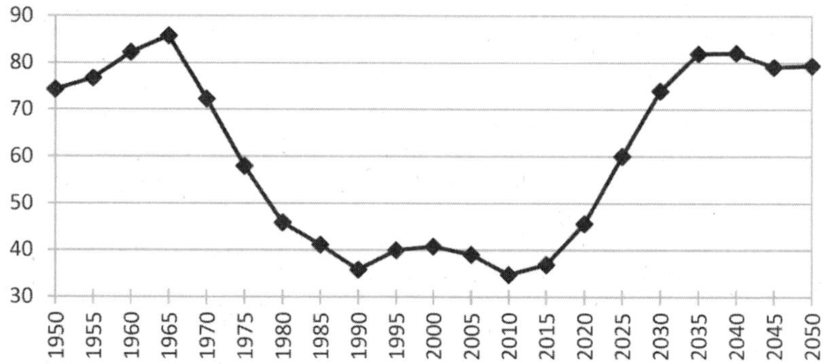


**Figure 1:** Singapore Age Dependency Ratio

*Note:* Figures from 2015 onwards are projections.
*Source:* United Nations Population Division.

While we know a lot about the impending rise in the ageing population and the challenges in the provision of support services, we are still at an early stage of evolving new societal arrangements to accommodate and take advantage of the skills and talents of this group of healthy and educated older persons. The future number and characteristics of the older persons have been projected regularly and were submitted and scrutinised by successive Ministerial Committees on Ageing. Yet, I am surprised how little we have done collectively to add meaning and fulfillment to the last 20 to 30 years of life of many older persons. Perhaps we are at the beginning of a process which will pick up momentum in time. I also believe that end-of-life issues will increasingly be discussed openly as this society confronts the challenges of an ageing population.

## The Birth Dearth

The current long-run fertility decline, which started in the 1970s, is well documented. The "Stop at Two" population policy might have facilitated a faster and more drastic decline. Nonetheless, the decline of Singapore's fertility is in line with the rest of the Asian cities. We have thus far been using the "Total Fertility Rate" (TFR) as the key indicator to track fertility trends. This indicator comprises of two components: the proportion of married women and the level of marital fertility. Over time, we have seen a delay in marriage timing and an associated decline in the absolute number of married women. The level of marital fertility has also declined, and therefore, the number of families with one or no children on the rise. The consequence of the combined effect is a sustained below-replacement TFR. These analyses were based on the data from periodic surveys and population censuses, and I think we have a good grasp of the level and trends, including period and cohort fertility.

The declining numbers of the resident births (births born to resident households) and the comparison between "resident births" and reported "total births" are shown in Figure 2. In the past 10 years, the number of resident births has been trending between 35,000 to 38,000, and the divergence between the "total" and "resident" births has become greater with more foreigners giving birth in Singapore. I am not sure why the Government continues to use the number of "total" births in some of the analysis which is quite misleading.

What is of concern is the successive stepwise decline in the size of the resident birth cohorts: an average cohort will be below 35,000 in the years to come. I do not believe anyone would agree that a cohort of 35,000 a year is sufficient to meet Singapore's manpower

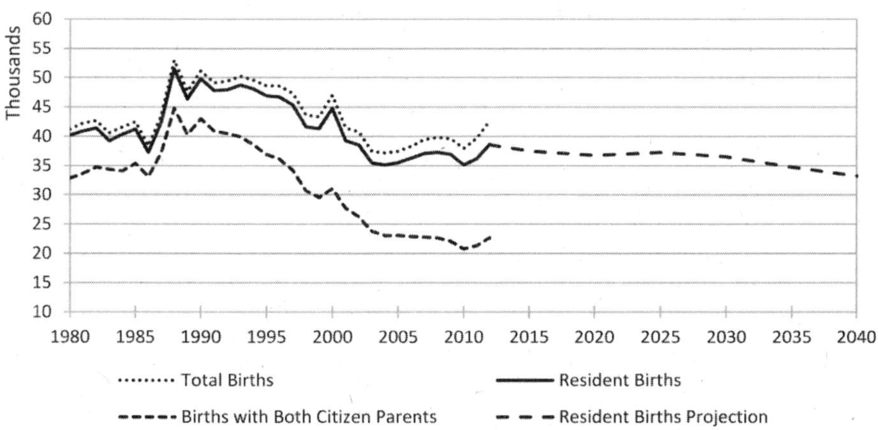


**Figure 2:** Total Number of Births

*Sources*: Singapore Demographic Bulletin; Immigration Checkpoints Authority.

needs. Moreover, what is of interest is that only 60 percent of the resident births are born to both parents who are citizens (around 25,000 per year). In other words, four out of 10 births are born to families, with at least one parent being a migrant. I am surprised by this change, as the proportion was much lower in the 1980s. This is in line with the marriage trends discussed below.

In Singapore, procreation occurs with a marriage and the family is often deemed as the most important social institution. Government policies have focused on supporting the functioning of the family in every aspect. However, the Singapore family is changing as well. Young Singaporean families of today are much better educated and globally mobile. What is the value of children to modern Singaporean family, today? Are two or three children still the ideal family size? I think we need a better understanding of this issue in order to appreciate the impact of changing values on the sustainability of Singaporean population. With the steady rise of childless or singleton families, I think we can expect Singaporean families to get even smaller in the future.

The nature of Singaporean families will also evolve due to compositional changes. Marriage to non-Singaporeans has been on the rise, reaching almost 40 percent of all Singaporean marriages. Figure 3 shows this rising trend of cross-national marriage. I am surprised by this trend which has important sociological implications. Is this a natural phenomenon as a result of increased contact with non-citizens locally or overseas? We know that the marriage bureaus play a role in arranging marriages for some Singaporeans with spouses from within the region. Will this trend stabilise at 40 percent or will it climb further? The data strongly suggest Singapore society has become more open or "globalised" than ever before. It would be very interesting to see how this globalisation trend would affect Singaporean family values, traditions and rituals.

A key consequence of the fertility and ageing trends is that the number of deaths will soon outstrip the number of births, resulting in a decline of our population size. The Government has projected that the natural increase for citizens will turn negative from about

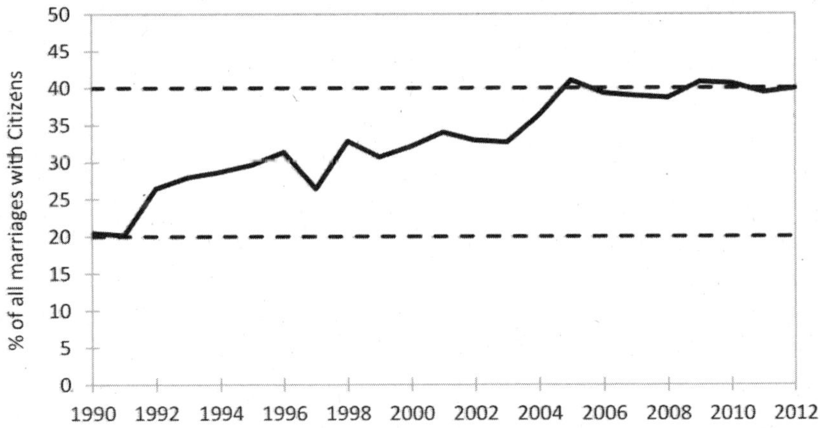


**Figure 3:** Proportion of Citizens Marrying Non-Citizens

*Source*: Department of Statistics.

2025 onwards and at that point, the citizen population will shrink. We have known this would happen since the 1970s; still, the fact that it will happen soon does bring a sense of foreboding. If we do allow more migrants to settle in Singapore as citizens, this will delay the onset of population decline. Objectively, this sounds like a rational choice. However, as in the case of Japan, there may be other considerations far more important than just balancing the numbers. Japan has stubbornly refused to go for an "easy" solution of importing labour (and citizens) to ease their population concerns. In contrast, we may have appeared to be too eager. While our choices may be limited as a small city-state, the volume and speed of absorption are policy variables that could have been more broadly discussed.

## Our Common Future

Our demographic trends are clear and supported by undisputed evidence. We know as a fact that we are heading towards a declining citizen population with an adverse age structure and rising dependency. This is our destiny. We will be dependent on migrant workers in the future in large numbers no matter how much we increase our productivity. During the 1980–2000 period, our development benefited from the "demographic dividend". The demand for foreign workers in this period was manageable. With the establishment of the National Productivity Board (NPB) and the push for higher "total factor productivity", there was reason to hope that foreign inflow will not be too large. The population projections prevailing at that time reflected this sentiment and assumed a much smaller foreign inflow, of about half to one million, to top up the citizen population. We assumed then that a steady state for the medium term could prevail with a four million population size.

In retrospect, I realise that the four million population projection in 1990 has grossly under-estimated the growth potential of Singapore and our capacity to accommodate a larger population. It is a no-brainer that population planning in Singapore must take full cognisance of Singapore's unique characteristics and constraints as a city-state. Some of the physical constraints have been minimised (such as new sources of water supply and land reclamation), and we know that with proper planning, Singapore has the capacity of supporting a much larger population with a high quality of life. The manpower needs have also surged due to favourable economic growth.

The current population projection issued by the Government in the White Paper has taken a factual assessment of the manpower needs of the future based on current economic scenarios, and has thus made a larger provision for population increase. Critics have argued that our future economic strategy must aim for "quality" growth with minimal dependency on foreign workers and a stronger push for productivity improvement. This is reasonable, and indeed "quality growth" rather than "growth at all costs" should be the guiding principle for future economic development. The Government has given some indications that a new economic strategy may indeed be required. There will however be a limit of how much we can substitute manpower by technology, and the fact remains that we critically need a foreign workforce to support and grow our economy.

Our demographic future will be shaped by how we perform on two key tasks. First, we have to continue to encourage the formation of Singaporean families to slow the decline of the population and to preserve our culture and traditions. The nature of Singaporean families will change, and it is unclear how the impact of cross-national marriages will erode traditional values and practices.

Secondly, we have to find an acceptable way to deal with future population inflows which will be sizeable. Our current population inflow is like "kueh lapis", with many layers forming a delicate structure. This structure of work permits and employment passes has been in existence for many years and our society has accepted it. Recent reactions to the inflow seem to focus on how foreigners have impacted the lives of Singaporeans. As the foreigners begin to form a critical mass in the labour market, Singaporeans feel that they are being squeezed out. Many Singaporeans feel that they are disadvantaged and even discriminated against in their home country. In addition, the sheer number of foreigners in common places such as markets, public transport, and food outlets gives rise to a feeling of being overwhelmed by outsiders.

I believe there is good understanding among Singaporeans of our population dynamics. The facts are not disputed. We know we need an inflow of foreigners to sustain our population and economy. However, we want this to be a managed inflow, with broader consultation on how the inflow should be managed. If Singaporeans continue to perceive that they have been squeezed out by the foreigners, this will bring forth broader political and sociological consequences. The Government must be seen to be advancing the interest of Singaporeans, rather than that of the foreigners. Unfortunately, this perception of a lack of "home-court" advantage is still widely held. The reactions to the White Paper on Population, the riot in Little India in 2013, the strike by bus drivers from China in 2012 — all these are signals that managing our future population growth will demand the Government to be far more attentive than ever on issues concerning the foreign workforce. The need to forge a public consensus on our manpower policy and the role of foreigners in our society is more apparent than ever before. We need this shared understanding and shared responsibility to meet the future demographic challenges and to sustain the growth and prosperity of our nation.

# Chapter 12

# Building an Enabling Environment for Successful Ageing*

*Susana Concordo Harding*

* This article was originally published in Commentary, Volume 25, titled "Singapore: A Democracy of Deeds and Problem-Solving" © 2016 The National University of Singapore Society. Susana Concordo Harding is Director, International Longevity Centre, and alumnus of the National University of Singapore, having completed her Master in Public Administration at its Lee Kuan Yew School of Public Policy.

Our founder, Mrs Tsao Ng Yu Shun, established the Tsao Foundation in 1993 to empower our elders and help them enjoy the opportunities for maximising personal growth, well-being and sense of fulfilment that longevity offers. In the early 1990s, Singapore was a very different place and concepts such as successful ageing and ageing in place were unheard of. In those days, the idea of home and community-based care for elders was new and the demographic concept of an ageing population was a relatively low-key subject.

Mrs Tsao had a very clear vision for the Tsao Foundation — of elders being supported and taken care of in their own homes by their families and loved ones, so that they can feel secure, surrounded by their families and continue to be in control of their lives. This is also the vision of her granddaughter, Dr Mary Ann Tsao, who translated and operationalised the vision by developing pioneering models of community-based health and social programmes as well as services to enable ageing in place and successful ageing; to empower mature adults to master their own ageing journey over the life course in terms of self-care and self-practice; and to access the right services at the right time.

## State and Civil Society on the Same Page on Ageing

By early 2000s, the landscape in Singapore had changed as it became a highly developed society. However, the issue of an ageing population was still a low-key subject and most of the community support for our elders was provided by voluntary welfare organisations (VWOs). There was also low awareness of the differential impact of ageing between men and women. It was against this backdrop that Dr Tsao, then President of the Foundation brought me into her team to lead in the advocacy work on two issues: first, women and ageing, and second, the participation of older people in community affairs.

In 2002, the United Nations (UN) General Assembly met in Spain and more than 160 UN member states debated and adopted the Madrid International Plan of Action on Ageing (MIPAA). Being sent to Madrid to witness this momentous event and to meet renowned leaders and experts in the field of ageing, was an excellent way to immerse myself in this sector and to start a career that has been both empowering and challenging to say the least.

Most of the time, the Singapore Government takes a cautious and prudent approach to signing and adopting international conventions and agreements. This, we understand is because it wishes to take its international commitments seriously and will only sign on to them if it is confident that it will benefit the Singaporean population and that it can implement commitments, policies and programmes effectively.

MIPAA, to a certain extent, was an exception in that Singapore signed on to it readily. I believe it was primarily because, as early as 1999, the Government had accepted the proposals by the first Inter-Ministerial Committee on Ageing (IMC, 1999). It is in this documented policy that the vision for the successful ageing for each and every Singaporean was stated and which the Government had already committed to, even before the UN General Assembly Meeting in Madrid took place.

## Creating a Senior-Friendly Community

Tsao Foundation continued to be the catalyst for creating change in the mindset of how people view and perceive ageing. The second decade of our work in the community focused on creating awareness of the differences between men and women as they grow older and how important it is to engage our elders and empower them so they can give their views and opinions on issues. We also had to ensure that we provide appropriate platforms so that they can participate in developing solutions for these issues.

It took the Foundation more than five years to demonstrate that older people can be engaged in the community through our "Voices for Older People" programme; that our older adults can be volunteers and ambassadors of the various active ageing programmes that we conduct and implement within the community; and that older people can learn about self-care through the Self-Care on Health of

Older Persons in Singapore (SCOPE) programme and change their health-seeking behaviour.

By 2009, Tsao Foundation had conceptualised and developed a community-wide public health planning approach to building an enabling environment for successful and active ageing in our communities — Community for Successful Ageing (ComSA). ComSA aims to enhance and rebuild the three systems that are critical for supporting older residents in the community to age well and to age in place. These systems consist of the following: integrated and comprehensive care system comprising primary care, care management and care service network; community development system comprising self-care and interest group formation, with focus on enhancing intergenerational solidarity; and infrastructural development comprising housing or residential facility and transport. The ComSA initiative shares the vision of the City for All Ages (CFAA) which aims to build senior-friendly communities where seniors can live safely and confidently, stay healthy and active, and be fully integrated (MSF, 2014).

In 2012, at the invitation of CFAA, Tsao Foundation decided to go to Whampoa and pilot test ComSA. By 2013, in partnership with CFAA Whampoa, the Ageing Planning Office of the Ministry of Health, the National Healthcare Group, and the Saw Swee Hock School of Public Health, we started to build a care system in the community through our person-centred primary care clinic and care management as well as service network amongst all health and social care providers in Whampoa. By 2014, we started implementing community development to facilitate successful ageing by effecting community-wide change through intergenerational dialogue and increased social cohesion among community members.

ComSA is giving Tsao Foundation a good opportunity to continue to be a catalyst that facilitates solution-building in Whampoa. As we get to know the community better, it has helped us identify other needs of the elders; provided us with ideas that we can work on together with our partners to effect change and impact how residents, especially our elders' experience of ageing in the community.

## A Brighter Future

The way ahead, I believe, is going to be slightly easier — not because we know all that there is to know on ageing successfully and maximising the potential and opportunities that greater longevity presents to Singapore, but rather because the new policies announced recently by the Government (Pioneer Generation Package and the $3 billion Action Plan to Enable Singaporeans to Age Successfully) will provide stronger support to VWOs and clearly signal that there is a strong commitment within the Government to act upon shared goals.

For the Foundation, our catalytic and thought leadership roles will continue as our work in empowering our elders through ComSA has just begun. Exciting times are ahead indeed for our elders and for all of us working alongside with them within the community.

# Chapter 13

# A Sustainable Future through Purposeful Making*

*Veerappan Swaminathan*

* This article was originally published in Commentary, Volume 25, titled "Singapore: A Democracy of Deeds and Problem-Solving" © 2016 The National University of Singapore Society. Veerappan Swaminathan is the Co-Founder of Sustainable Living Lab, a social innovation lab that harnesses the energy of the Maker Movement to build a sustainable future.

Ensuring the sustainability of our society and species is perhaps the biggest challenge of our times. The science about the adverse impact of mankind's activities on the environment has been clear since the seventies. Yet no significant action, beyond numerous ineffective global meetings, has been taken to mitigate, much less reverse the decline.

Today, we can see clear evidence of the environmental effects — fast receding polar ice caps, declining fish stocks and erratic weather patterns which are leading to socio-economic issues such as lack of access to clean water, worsening land and air pollution, and increasing rural-urban income inequality.

Having been born into the generation that will likely bear the brunt of these effects, the options before me as I thought about it while I was at university, was either to be a driver of change or be a passenger of fate.

## Three Pillars of Sustainability

It was in response to these global challenges that a group of my course mates at the National University of Singapore (NUS) and I founded the Sustainable Living Lab (SL2) with the vision of building a sustainable future through practical action.

We started out as a student club at NUS in 2009 and then transitioned into a social enterprise in 2011.

Sustainability is often viewed within the scope of the environment, but we took a broader view as we felt that a sustainable future can only be achieved if we considered the interconnectedness of the environment, society and the economy — commonly referred to as the "Three Pillars Model of Sustainability" by experts and practitioners in this field.

In this model, the environment represents a finite boundary within which human society and the economy exist. The economy is viewed as a subset of society with the reasoning that it is derived from society or created by it to efficiently exchange value within most, although not with all elements of society. Those that create

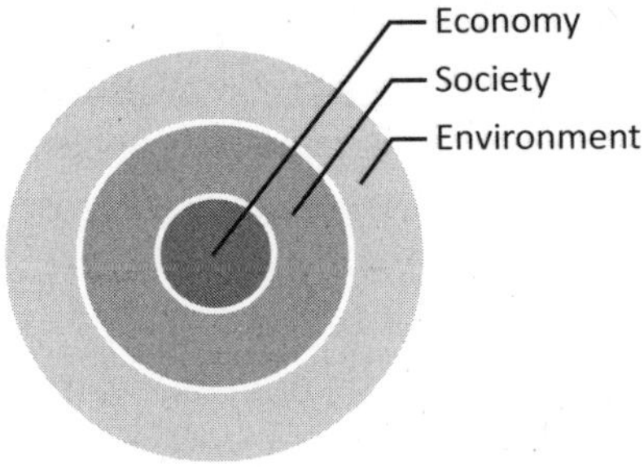


social value without going through the market are, for example, stay-at-home mums and other caregivers.

However, the reality is that we tend to give outsized attention and dedicate immense resources to the economy, with society being deemed as being of secondary importance and the environment, often relegated to an occasional concern.

Building a sustainable future means taking into consideration all three pillars — environmental, social and economic sustainability — because they are interconnected and cannot be meaningfully separated.

Ultimately, a sustainable future is one in which we can continue to thrive as a species without negatively impacting the opportunities for our future generations to flourish.

## Coming Home to Roost

In Singapore, our national leaders have, since Independence, prioritised the attainment of economic sustainability as the primary strategy for achieving national progress. They were careful to incorporate positive environmental practices such as banning or regulating polluting industries, enforcing the installation of catalytic converters in motorcars and embarking on a national tree planting programme. These practices ensured that Singapore itself remained liveable as we made rapid economic progress. However, we have to recognise this has still come at a price which we may soon have to pay.

On the environmental front, our extensive land reclamation policies have resulted in sand export bans from Malaysia, Indonesia and Vietnam with accusations of environmental degradation coming from Cambodia- and Myanmar-based environmental organisations. Another problem is the financing and growth of the palm oil and paper pulp industry by Singapore-linked companies, that some evidence suggests, are culpable through their supply chains for forest fires, massive deforestation and habitat loss for indigenous animal species in Indonesia. The yearly transboundary haze serves as an annual reminder of our complicity in the environmental degradation of our neighbours.

On the social front, we have an increasing income divide, leading to reduced social mobility which threatens the belief in meritocracy as a key organising principle in our governance system.

On the economic front, our continuing heavy reliance on the oil refining industry for jobs and economic growth also makes it difficult to truly commit to a shift towards renewable energy. While what was primarily an "economy-first" strategy may have worked for Singapore in its early years, it is clear that if we are to look forward to continued progress as a nation, environmental and social concerns will have to take on greater prominence.

We recognise though, that the sustainability challenge has every feature of a classic "wicked problem", with multiple interconnected causes that interact with each other. To make matters even more challenging, the transboundary nature of sustainability issues puts any solution out of reach of any single state actor. Any nation choosing to take unilateral action rightfully fears that if others do not follow their lead, their actions will be pointless or worse still, may end up backfiring if their country becomes side-lined in the community of nations. For a country such as Singapore, which is heavily dependent on other nations but also relatively small in its ability to significantly change any situation, taking unilateral action is understandably viewed as a non-option. Pragmatic thinking suggests that we are and will remain a "price-taker" and not a "price-setter" at the international stage in so many respects. Judging by how the international community has actually been "setting the price" over the last few decades, it will be unwise to expect any major global reform regarding sustainability in the near term.

Interestingly, this is not the first time in our national history that we have encountered such bleak circumstances which seemed beyond our control. At the birth of our nation in 1965, in response to the hostile neighbourhood we found ourselves in, our leaders used every ounce of ingenuity they could muster to engage in a dual policy of shoring up our defence capabilities (by instituting National Service for instance) and engaging in intense diplomacy to allow Singapore to punch above its weight on the world stage. This would not have been possible if our society had not possessed the never-say-die attitude and gumption to tackle challenges head-on.

## The Maker Mindset

Similar doggedness, resolve and creativity are required of all of us today. At SL2, we feel that sustainability challenges are among the issues that are beyond the scope and capacity of national governments to address. In an era where the influence of multinational corporations is growing, with the economic value they generate sometimes even surpassing that of nation-states, a strategy of addressing sustainability challenges through socially-driven enterprises could offer better dividends. Setting up social enterprises only solves one part of the problem; that is, providing an engine to drive us towards sustainability. As a society, we also need to internalise the interconnectedness of our environmental, social and economic systems and develop a global culture of sharing and collaboration. This is where the Maker Movement comes in.

The Maker Movement came into prominence globally in 2006 as a result of several intersecting driving forces — widespread Internet access; low-cost Chinese manufacturing; popularity of open source hardware designs; expiry of key technology patents; a trend towards self-actualisation amongst young people; and a yearning for tactile experiences by a generation who are great at using technology but very poor in understanding how it is made.

While the Maker Movement is often associated with technological advances, what is far less obvious is that it promotes a unique mindset — the Maker Mindset — which indicates a common set of behaviours observed amongst Makers. Allow me to explain.

Makers come in all shapes and sizes with some being hobbyists and others operating as professionals, but all of them utilising technology and ingenuity, in equal parts, to engage in developing new products and services. Makers, regardless of where they hail from, tend to possess a "growth mindset", practice craftsmanship values and believe in "open sharing". The "growth mindset", a concept popularised by Carol Dweck, refers to the personal belief that intelligence is not fixed and that one can learn any new subject matter. As you can imagine, this is a particularly empowering belief system and explains why Makers are so comfortable working with ambiguity as they explore new technologies and methods.

Any skilled person has to go through years of careful practice to improve their craft and that is the same with Makers. Bear in mind that in Singapore, at the time of writing, there is no diploma offered for being a Maker, so the process of attaining mastery depends less on formal training, more on peer-sharing and the heavy investment of one's time and effort. Makers put in that effort due to the intrinsic motivation of wanting to produce one's best work independent of any reward or praise. That is not all. If the acquisition of mastery is not tempered with humility and grace, it can easily result in pride. The practice of "open sharing" in the Maker community grounds the Maker and reflects a realisation that humanity stands taller on the shoulder of giants — that ideas multiply and not diminish through sharing.

Given the complex nature of sustainability issues, seeking and assimilating knowledge in cooperation with many others is par for the course to make any sort of dent. In our opinion, the traits exhibited by Makers are exactly the sort we need people to develop if society is to successfully address and overcome complex sustainability challenges.

## Purposeful Making

As an organisation, we adopted the ethos of the Maker Movement and focused our work on inspiring and directing the creative energy of Makers towards building a sustainable future.

Our work involves generating positive social capital through friendships and peer-sharing, protecting the natural environment and creating economic activity that is conducive for sustainable human development. We call this "Purposeful Making".

Let me illustrate what I have said by sharing with you several projects that SL2 has engaged in and the impact that has resulted from these.

## Social Sustainability

In our view, the first order of business in tackling the complex issues of sustainability is to identify like-minded individuals, develop their potential and build a community of practice around them. Every community needs a physical space to do that in, hence we pioneered the development of "makerspaces" in Singapore, starting the first such facility in 2011 at the former Bottle Tree Park in Yishun.

Makerspaces are zones of self-directed learning, which are equipped with the latest in technology, other resources and creative tools such as 3D printers, laser cutters, computerised milling machines, sewing stations and circuit board printers, along with the educational resources for users of the space to gain familiarity with the various tools.

They serve as a node or a magnet (depending on how you look at it) for a community of Makers to gather around a common intent (in our case, addressing sustainability challenges) to foster a highly collaborative, action-biased dynamic through a culture of mutual peer support, advice and assistance.

In our case, this conducive environment was our first step in giving the public a platform to engage in purposeful making and it allowed the team to develop other programmes and products such as "Future Fridays", "Repair Kopitiam" and the invention of the "iBam", all of which I elaborate upon later.

In 2014, we were also fortunate to be part of a consortium that successfully won the bid to develop a Prototyping Centre — a Makerspace to promote tinkering and hardware entrepreneurship — at the National Design Centre. Having learned from our experience which we shared widely in the mass media and through hosting numerous local and foreign visitors, many educational institutions and private makerspaces have set up in Singapore and the region by other parties.

Interestingly, many Southeast Asian makerspaces have been organised around the aim of addressing local social issues or sustainability challenges which is very unlike the makerspaces that can be found in the United States or Europe. We would like to think that we had a hand in influencing that change!

However, having a physical facility alone is not enough. A shift towards sustainable thinking is only possible when people are interested in thinking and acting for the long term, so the next order of business, it was clear to us, was to create a mindset change around sustainability. It was with that intention that we initiated "Future Fridays".

The premise of Future Fridays is simple: it is to equip working professionals with the knowledge and practice of futures-thinking tools, so that they can influence change towards sustainable practices within their own organisations.

These sessions which take place regularly on Friday evenings focus on a wide range of topics — from the Future of Work to the Future of Transport and even the Future of Food in an effort to demonstrate the interconnectedness of nearly any issue with the larger one of sustainability. The sessions help participants to think systematically of scenarios of the future around the selected topic. The sessions end with participants manifesting their ideas for a preferred sustainable future in the form of physical artefacts that they create. These artefacts are exhibited at the makerspace or other prominent locations to activate public conversations around the issue of sustainability.

It is heartening to note that we have had many corporate partners and civil society organisations get involved in thinking through their current strategies in the context of long-term trends that might affect their sectors. For example, several local food sustainability groups collaborated after participating in a Future Fridays session. They organised a huge "meetup" of the different players in the food ecosystem to address the sustainability of food supply in Singapore.

Seeding change in mindset around sustainability takes time, but we believe it is already paying dividends as we see the nature of strategic conversations change to accommodate long-term thinking on the issue even among smaller organisations.

## Environmental Sustainability

Where the first two initiatives — Makerspaces and Future Fridays — dealt primarily with the development of positive social capital as well as a mindset change around sustainability, the "Repair Kopitiam" project dealt with the widespread environmental issue of waste generation in Singapore.

Despite decades of awareness-building and educational efforts, the amount of waste that is generated keeps increasing largely due to the "buy-and-throw-away" culture — an outcome of consumer affluence in Singapore.

Inspired by the Repair Cafes of Europe, we devised the Repair Kopitiam programme as an effort to tackle this buy-and-throw-away culture in a way that seeks to prevent waste in the first place and revolves around practical action. First, we teach volunteers how to repair electrical home appliances, furniture and fabrics. We then have our newly-minted "Repair Coaches" conduct public repair programmes at high traffic void decks of public housing flats to teach members of the public how to repair their own broken items. These public sessions, which attract up to 300 members of the public each time, are conducted every last Sunday of the month through our roster of over 60 repair coaches. We estimate that our participants now repair about 60 percent of all items that are broken and are therefore saved from the trash heap. At the sessions, participants or those who are just gawking often just mingle around with their neighbours and enjoy a cup of coffee on us — hence we call it Repair Kopitiam.

Participants, most of whom are below 20 years of age and above 40, often share that they were attracted to the Repair Kopitiam sessions not because of environmental reasons but because it seemed like a fun and social way to spend a Sunday morning. This concept of "incidental environmentalism" is something that we seek to manifest in all our programmes as we want to reach an audience that is traditionally indifferent to environmental messaging. Often times, it is not necessary for people to be fully aware that they are engaging in an environmental practice. What is more important is that they actually practise environmentally-friendly habits — never mind what their primary intention might be.

Today, many corporate and educational institutions have started to adopt repair activities into their basket of environmental corporate social responsibility programmes alongside the usual recycling programmes and litter-picking activities.

We have also expanded the Repair Kopitiam programme to include performing repair activities at several voluntary welfare organisations that typically have many wheelchairs and equipment for seniors that require maintenance but might otherwise be sent to the waste dump due to the lack of professional repair services. Our ultimate aim is for people to always consider if an item can be repaired and restored before sending it off to the trash heap.

## Economic Sustainability

The final pillar of sustainability has to do with building an economy that is conducive for, and not at the expense of, human development. When it comes to addressing sustainability issues, many companies view it from a compliance perspective or from a corporate social responsibility perspective. We feel that there is a third way — sustainability can be seen as an impetus for innovation; a way to unlock or create new economic value.

When we created our popular bamboo sound amplifiers for iPhones and the like — called iBam — we took great care to ensure that the process of harvesting, manufacturing and packaging was done in a manner that reduced harm on the environment and created opportunities for vulnerable communities to remain employed. Traditional craftsmen from the declining *angklung* (a traditional Indonesian musical instrument) sector were re-employed to use their specialist skills in manufacturing the iBams and the packaging was stitched from raw unbleached cotton by stay-at-home single mothers in Singapore.

When it comes to traditional economic activity, much of it operates on a linear model which starts from raw material extraction and at the end of its useful shelf-life, ends up in the dump. Today, new models of sharing spare capacity have greatly impacted the hotel industry (AirBnB), transport industry (Uber, Grab, GoGoVan etc.) and the commercial property sector in the form of shared co-working offices.

All of these trends are part of a move towards an economy that is more circular in nature — a product can be shared as a service, be easily repaired, remanufactured as good as new or is extremely easy to separate so as to recover valuable constituent materials. In fact it could be said that the "circular economy" is perhaps the new model of an economy that can take-off in the context of the massive sustainability challenges we are facing.

## Conclusion

The initiatives of SL2 that have been mentioned are just some of the ways we manifest the concept of purposeful making in daily practice.

Clearly much more work is needed on all levels of society if we are to be able to overcome the tough times ahead for our society and even Planet Earth. There are positive signs and reasons for optimism out there though. I am continually surprised by how much young people know about sustainability issues and by their efforts to engage in meaningful work in this area. I have also been encouraged by the actions taken by some prominent mainstream organisations to fundamentally change the way they have been going about their business and operating in ways that are more in tune with the resource-constrained world we are a part of.

As Mahatma Gandhi once said, "The world has enough for everyone's need, but not enough for everyone's greed".